Our Songs

A hymn book for Catholic schools

kevin
mayhew

kevin
mayhew

First published in Great Britain in 1998 by Kevin Mayhew Ltd.
Buxhall, Stowmarket, Suffolk IP14 3BW
Tel: +44 (0) 1449 737978   Fax: +44 (0) 1449 737834
E-mail: info@kevinmayhew.com

www.kevinmayhew.com

9 8 7 6 5 4 3 2 1

Words
ISBN 978 1 84003 165 2
ISMN M 57004 331 6
Catalogue No. 1413071

Full Music
ISBN 978 1 84003 164 5
ISMN M 57004 249 4
Catalogue No. 1413074

Front cover: *Crowd* by Judy Byford reproduced by courtesy of SuperStock, London.
Cover design by Jaquetta Sergeant
Typesetting by Louise Selfe

Printed and bound in Great Britain

Acknowledgements

The publishers wish to express their gratitude to the copyright holders who have granted permission to include their material in this book.

Every effort has been made to trace the copyright holders of all the songs in this collection and we hope that no copyright has been infringed. Apology is made and pardon sought if the contrary be the case, and a correction will be made in any reprint of this book.

For additional information on the copyright holders please contact the Copyright Department at Kevin Mayhew Ltd (copyright@kevinmayhew.com)

Important Copyright Information

We would like to remind users of this songbook that the reproduction of any song texts or music without the permission of the copyright holder is illegal. Details of all copyright holders are clearly indicated below each song.

Most of the song texts are covered by a Christian Copyright Licensing (CCL) licence. If you possess a CCL licence, it is essential that you check your instruction manual to ensure that the song you wish to use is covered.

If you are not a member of CCLI, or the song you wish to reproduce is not covered by your licence, you must contact the copyright holder direct for their permission.

Christian Copyright Licensing International (CCLI) have also now introduced a Music Reproduction Licence. Again, if you hold such a licence it is essential that you check your instruction manual to ensure that the song you wish to reproduce is covered. The reproduction of any music not covered by your licence is both illegal and immoral.

If you are interested in joining CCLI they can be contacted at the following address:

**CCLI, Chantry House, 22 Upperton Road,
Eastbourne East Sussex, BN21 1BF.**

Tel: 01323 436100, www.ccli.co.uk

Alternatively, a large proportion of the songs in this book are covered by the **Calamus Licence**. If you hold this licence and would like to use any of the song texts, please refer to your membership information or contact Nicholas Blackford at Calamus nicholas@decanimusic.co.uk. Please ensure that you include these songs in your Annual Licence Quarterly Usage Report sheet, within the year covered by the licence.

If you would like to join the Calamus UK Copyright Scheme or are unsure of whether the songs that you wish to use are covered by this licence, please contact them either by telephone on **01842 819830** or by email, **nicholas@decanimusic.co.uk**. More information can be found on their website: **www.decanimusic.co.uk**

Foreword

Dear Children

The songs in this book have a simple message –
that God loves you,
all the time and everywhere!
He also loves everyone else in the world,
and because he made the world,
he loves that too.

Wouldn't it be wonderful
if we could love everyone and everything
the way God does,
so that there would be no more bullying,
quarrels, fighting or wars?
That might not happen straight away
but we can make a start on it right now,
wherever we are.

Happy singing!

KEVIN MAYHEW
Editor

Contents

GENERAL HYMNS

General Hymns

1   Carey Landry

Abba, Abba, Father.
You are the potter,
we are the clay,
the work of your hands.

1. Mould us, mould us and fashion us
   into the image of Jesus, your Son,
   of Jesus, your Son.

2. Father, may we be one in you,
   as he is in you and you are in him,
   and you are in him.

3. Glory, glory and praise to you,
   glory and praise to you for ever, amen,
   for ever, amen.

2   Dave Bilbrough

Abba, Father, let me be
yours and yours alone.
May my will for ever be
more and more your own.
Never let my heart grow cold,
never let me go.
Abba, Father, let me be
yours and yours alone.

3 Virginia Vissing

1. Abba, Father, send your Spirit,
   glory, Jesus Christ.
   Abba, Father, send your Spirit,
   glory, Jesus Christ.

   Glory, hallelujah,
   glory, Jesus Christ.
   Glory, hallelujah,
   glory, Jesus Christ.

2. If you seek me, you will find me,
   glory, Jesus Christ.
   If you seek me, you will find me,
   glory, Jesus Christ.

3. If you listen, you will hear me,
   glory, Jesus Christ.
   If you listen, you will hear me,
   glory, Jesus Christ.

4 Carey Landry

Lines in ordinary type are sung by the leader; those in bold type by everybody.

1. A butterfly,
   a butterfly,
   an Easter egg,
   an Easter egg,
   a fountain flowing in the park
   a fountain flowing in the park.

These are signs of new life;
the life of Jesus the Lord.
And we sing to him, alleluia!
We give to him our praise!
We sing to him, alleluia!
Glory be to him!
Glory be to him!
Glory be to Jesus the Lord!

2. A helping hand,
   a helping hand,
   a happy smile,
   a happy smile,
   a heart so full of hope and joy,
   a heart so full of hope and joy.

3. A cup of wine,
   a cup of wine,
   a loaf of bread,
   a loaf of bread,
   now blest and broken for us all,
   now blest and broken for us all.

5   Hayward Osborne

1. All creation, bless the Lord.
   Earth and heaven, bless the Lord.
   Spirits, powers, bless the Lord.
   Praise him for ever.
   Sun and moon, bless the Lord.
   Stars and planets, bless the Lord.
   Dews and showers, bless the Lord.
   Praise him for ever.

Continued overleaf

2. Winds and breezes, bless the Lord.
   Spring and autumn, bless the Lord.
   Winter, summer, bless the Lord.
   Praise him for ever.
   Fire and heat, bless the Lord.
   Frost and cold, bless the Lord.
   Ice and snow, bless the Lord.
   Praise him for ever.

3. Night and daytime, bless the Lord.
   Light and darkness, bless the Lord.
   Clouds and lightning, bless the Lord.
   Praise him for ever.
   All the earth, bless the Lord.
   Hills and mountains, bless the Lord.
   Trees and flowers, bless the Lord.
   Praise him for ever.

4. Springs and rivers, bless the Lord.
   Seas and oceans, bless the Lord.
   Whales and fishes, bless the Lord.
   Praise him for ever.
   Birds and insects, bless the Lord.
   Beasts and cattle, bless the Lord.
   Let all creatures bless the Lord.
   Praise him for ever.

5. Let God's people bless the Lord.
   Men and women, bless the Lord.
   All creation, bless the Lord.
   Praise him for ever.
   Let God's people bless the Lord.
   Men and women, bless the Lord.
   All creation, bless the Lord.
   Praise him for ever.

6 William Henry Draper, alt.

1. All creatures of our God and King,
   lift up your voice and with us sing,
   O praise him, alleluia!
   Thou burning sun with golden beam,
   thou silver moon with softer gleam,

   O praise him, O praise him,
   alleluia, alleluia, alleluia.

2. Let all things their Creator bless,
   and worship him in humbleness,
   O praise him, alleluia!
   Praise, praise the Father, praise the Son,
   and praise the Spirit, Three in One.

© 1996 J. Curwen & Sons Ltd.

7 Unknown/Damian Lundy

1. Alleluia, alleluia,
   alleluia, alleluia,
   alleluia, alleluia,
   alleluia, alleluia.

2. Jesus is Lord,
   Jesus is Lord,
   Jesus is Lord,
   Jesus is Lord.

3. And I love him,
   and I love him,
   and I love him,
   and I love him.

Continued overleaf

4. Christ is risen,
   Christ is risen,
   Christ is risen,
   Christ is risen.

*Additional verses may be composed to suit the occasion.
For example:*

5. Send your Spirit . . .

6. Abba, Father . . .

7. Come, Lord Jesus . . .

© *1977 Kevin Mayhew Ltd.*

8 Donald Fishel

*Alleluia, alleluia,
give thanks to the risen Lord,
alleluia, alleluia,
give praise to his name.*

1. Jesus is Lord of all the earth,
   he is the King of creation.

2. Spread the good news o'er all the earth,
   Jesus has died and has risen.

3. Come, let us praise the living God,
   joyfully sing to our Saviour.

© *1973 Word of God Music/CopyCare*

9 Hubert J. Richards

Solo: *Alleluia, alleluia.*
All: *Alleluia, alleluia.*
Solo: *Alleluia,*
All: *alleluia.*

1. All the earth, sing out to the Lord.
   Serve the Lord with joy in your heart;
   come into his presence with song.

2. Come and bring your gifts to the Lord.
   Come before him, singing his praise;
   He is Lord, and he is our God.

3. God is good, his love never ends;
   he is always true to his word,
   he is faithful, age upon age.

10 Traditional

Alleluia, alleluia,
alleluia, alleluia.

11 Scripture

Alleluia, alleluia,
alleluia, alleluia!

Speak, Lord, your servant is listening:
you have the message of eternal life.

12 Joe Wise

Alleluia, alleluia,
alleluia, alleluia,
alleluia.

We will hear your Word, one in love;
we will live your Word, one in love;
we will spread your Word, one in love.

13 Peter Watcyn-Jones

1. All God's people, come together,
   worship the King!
   For his love will last for ever,
   worship the King!
   Through life's struggles he'll be with us,
   he'll be guiding, watching o'er us.
   We rejoice, sing hallelujah,
   Worship the King!

2. All God's people, pray together,
   peace to the world!
   Loving brother, loving sister,
   peace to the world!
   God is love and God is kindness,
   he will guide us through the darkness.
   We rejoice, sing hallelujah,
   peace to the world!

3. All God's people, love each other,
    glory to God!
    Though we die we live for ever,
    glory to God!
    We will enter life eternal,
    chosen, blessed, for ever praising.
    We rejoice, sing hallelujah,
    glory to God!

14   Traditional

1. All in an Easter garden,
    before the break of day,
    an angel came from heaven
    and rolled the stone away.
    When Jesus' friends came seeking,
    with myrrh and spices rare,
    they found the angels at the door,
    but Jesus was not there.

2. All in an Easter garden,
    where water lilies bloom,
    the angels gave their message
    beside an empty tomb:
    'The Lord is here no longer,
    come, see where once he lay;
    the Lord of life is ris'n indeed,
    for this is Easter Day.'

15 Spiritual

All night, all day,
angels watchin' over me, my Lord.
All night, all day,
angels watchin' over me.

1. Day is dyin' in the west,
   angels watchin' over me, my Lord.
   Sleep, my child, and take your rest,
   angels watchin' over me.

2. Now I lay me down to sleep,
   angels watchin' over me, my Lord.
   Pray the Lord my soul to keep,
   angels watchin' over me.

16 Doug Marks-Smirchirch

All of my heart, all of my soul,
all of my mind, all of my strength.
(Repeat)
With everything within me
I want to praise you, Lord.
I want to love you with all that I am,
and bring joy to your heart.

Last time:
Let me bring joy to your heart all of my life.

© *Right on the Mark Music/Copyright Control*

17 Michael Forster

1. All of the creatures God had made
   came to the ark, a big parade,
   walked up the gangplank, two by two,
   'Coo!' said the doves, 'it's a floating zoo!'

2. Everything seemed to come in pairs,
   camels and dogs and big brown bears;
   Noah said to God, 'It's rather rough;
   one of the fleas would be quite enough.'

3. All huddled up in one small space,
   one of the dogs said, 'What a place!
   I haven't room to swing a cat!'
   'Well,' said the cat, 'thank the Lord for that!'

4. People are often like that, too,
   living in boxes, two by two.
   We have to learn to get along,
   just like the animals in this song.

18 Susan Sayers

All of the people on the mountain,
all of the people in the valley,
all of the people in the villages and the town,
say to each other on the way,
'Bring all your friends and don't delay,
Jesus of Nazareth is coming here today.'

1. Jesus, Jesus, when we are with you,
   it's strange, and yet it's true,
   we start to feel that there is
   more to life than living as we do.
   It's richer and more satisfying
   than we ever knew.

Continued overleaf

2. Jesus, Jesus, healing as you go,
   your loving seems to flow
   like water from a fountain,
   and as we are touched we want to grow
   in love towards each other –
   just because you love us so!

   All of the people on the mountain,
   all of the people in the valley,
   all of the people in the villages and the town,
   say to each other on the way,
   'Bring all your friends and don't delay,
   Jesus of Nazareth is coming here today.'

3. Jesus, Jesus, we have come to see
   that you must really be
   the Son of God our Father.
   We've been with you and we all agree
   that only in your service
   can the world be truly free!

19 Roy Turner

1. All over the world the Spirit is moving,
   all over the world,
   as the prophets said it would be.
   All over the world
   there's a mighty revelation
   of the glory of the Lord,
   as the waters cover the sea.

2. All over this land the Spirit is moving,
   all over this land,
   as the prophets said it would be.
   All over this land
   there's a mighty revelation
   of the glory of the Lord,
   as the waters cover the sea.

3. All over the Church the Spirit is moving,
   all over the Church,
   as the prophets said it would be.
   All over the Church
   there's a mighty revelation
   of the glory of the Lord,
   as the waters cover the sea.

4. All over us all the Spirit is moving,
   all over us all,
   as the prophets said it would be.
   All over us all
   there's a mighty revelation
   of the glory of the Lord,
   as the waters cover the sea.

5. Deep down in my heart the Spirit is moving,
   deep down in my heart,
   as the prophets said it would be.
   Deep down in my heart
   there's a mighty revelation
   of the glory of the Lord,
   as the waters cover the sea.

20 Sebastian Temple

1. All that I am, all that I do,
   all that I'll ever have I offer now to you.
   Take and sanctify these gifts
   for your honour, Lord.
   Knowing that I love and serve you
   is enough reward.
   All that I am, all that I do,
   all that I'll ever have I offer now to you.

2. All that I dream, all that I pray,
   all that I'll ever make I give to you today.
   Take and sanctify these gifts
   for your honour, Lord.
   Knowing that I love and serve you
   is enough reward.
   All that I am, all that I do,
   all that I'll ever have I offer now to you.

21 Bob Dufford

All the ends of the earth,
all you creatures of the sea,
lift up your eyes to the wonders of the Lord.
For the Lord of the earth,
the Master of the sea,
has come with justice for the world.

1. Break into song at the deeds of the Lord,
   the wonders he has done in every age.

2. Heaven and earth shall rejoice in his might:
   every heart, every nation call him Lord.

3. The Lord has made his salvation known,
   faithful to his promises of old.
   Let the sea of the earth,
   let the sea and all it holds
   make music before our King!

22 Michael Cockett

All the nations of the earth,
praise the Lord who brings to birth
the greatest star, the smallest flow'r.
Alleluia.

1. Let the heavens praise the Lord,
   alleluia.
   Moon and stars, praise the Lord,
   alleluia.

2. Snow-capped mountains, praise the Lord,
   alleluia.
   Rolling hills, praise the Lord,
   alleluia.

3. Deep sea water, praise the Lord,
   alleluia.
   Gentle rain, praise the Lord,
   alleluia.

4. Roaring lion, praise the Lord,
   alleluia.
   Singing birds, praise the Lord,
   alleluia.

Continued overleaf

5. Earthly monarchs, praise the Lord,
   alleluia.
   Young and old, praise the Lord,
   alleluia.

   All the nations of the earth,
   praise the Lord who brings to birth
   the greatest star, the smallest flow'r.
   Alleluia.

23 Cecil Frances Alexander

All things bright and beautiful,
all creatures great and small,
all things wise and wonderful,
the Lord God made them all.

1. Each little flow'r that opens,
   each little bird that sings,
   he made their glowing colours,
   he made their tiny wings.

2. The purple-headed mountain,
   the river running by,
   the sunset and the morning
   that brightens up the sky.

3. The cold wind in the winter,
   the pleasant summer sun,
   the ripe fruits in the garden,
   he made them every one.

4. He gave us eyes to see them,
   and lips that we might tell
   how great is God almighty
   who has made all things well.

24 Unknown

And everyone beneath the vine and fig tree
shall live in peace and have no fear.
And everyone beneath the vine and fig tree
shall live in peace and have no fear.
And into ploughshares turn their swords,
nations shall learn war no more.
And into ploughshares turn their swords,
nations shall learn war no more.

25 Unknown

A new commandment
I give unto you:
that you love one another
as I have loved you,
that you love one another
as I have loved you.
By this shall all know
that you are my disciples,
if you have love one for another.
By this shall all know
that you are my disciples
if you have love one for another.

26 Barbara Ryberg

Anytime, anywhere,
I can talk to God.
When I'm glad, when I'm sad,
I can talk to God.
Sometimes on my knees I pray,
sometimes as I work or play,
when I need him through the day,
he is my best friend.

27 Anne Conway

1. As earth that is dry
   and parched in the sun
   lies waiting for rain,
   my soul is a desert,
   arid and waste;
   it longs for your word, O Lord.

   Come to the waters,
   all you who thirst,
   come, now, and eat my bread.

2. Though you have no money,
   come, buy my corn
   and drink my red wine.
   Why spend precious gold
   on what will not last?
   Hear me, and your soul will live.

3. As one on a journey
   strays from the road
   and falls in the dark,
   my mind is a wand'rer,
   choosing wrong paths
   and longing to find a star.

4. The Lord is your light,
   the Lord is your strength,
   turn back to him now,
   for his ways are not
   the ways you would choose,
   and his thoughts are always new.

5. As rain from the mountains
   falls on the land
   and brings forth the seed,
   the word of the Lord
   sinks deep in our hearts,
   creating the flow'r of truth.

28 Maria Parkinson

1. As I kneel before you,
   as I bow my head in prayer,
   take this day, make it yours
   and fill me with your love.

   Ave, Maria, gratia plena,
   Dominus tecum, benedicta tu.

Continued overleaf

2. All I have I give you,
   every dream and wish are yours;
   mother of Christ, mother of mine,
   present them to my Lord.

   Ave, Maria, gratia plena,
   Dominus tecum, benedicta tu.

3. As I kneel before you,
   and I see your smiling face,
   every thought, every word
   is lost in your embrace.

29 Martin Nystrom

1. As the deer pants for the water,
   so my soul longs after you.
   You alone are my heart's desire
   and I long to worship you.

   You alone are my strength, my shield,
   to you alone may my spirit yield.
   You alone are my heart's desire
   and I long to worship you.

2. I want you more than gold or silver,
   only you can satisfy.
   You alone are the real joy-giver
   and the apple of my eye.

3. You're my friend and you're my brother,
   even though you are a king.
   I love you more than any other,
   so much more than anything.

30 Jancis Harvey

1. A still small voice in the heart of the city,
   a still small voice on the mountain,
   through the storms that are raging
   or the quiet of the evening,
   it can only be heard if you listen.

2. The voice of God in a place that is troubled,
   the voice of God in the dawning,
   through the noise of the shouting,
   through the stillness of the sleeping,
   it can only be heard if you listen.

3. Give time to hear, give us love that will listen,
   give wisdom for understanding,
   there's a voice of stillness
   that to each of us is speaking,
   it can only be heard if you listen.

© Jancis Harvey

31 Anne Conway

1. Be still and know I am with you,
   be still, I am the Lord.
   I will not leave you orphans.
   I leave with you my world.

2. You fear the light may be fading,
   you fear to lose your way.
   Be still, and know I am near you.
   I'll lead you to the day and the sun.

Continued overleaf

3. Be glad the day you have sorrow,
   be glad, for then you live.
   The stars shine only in darkness,
   and in your need I give my peace.

32 Unknown

1. Be still and know that I am God,
   be still and know that I am God,
   be still and know that I am God.

2. In you, O Lord, I put my trust,
   in you, O Lord, I put my trust,
   in you, O Lord, I put my trust.

33 David J. Evans

1. Be still, for the presence of the Lord,
   the Holy One, is here.
   Come, bow before him now
   with reverence and fear.
   In him no sin is found,
   we stand on holy ground.
   Be still, for the presence of the Lord,
   the Holy One, is here.

2. Be still, for the glory of the Lord
   is shining all around;
   he burns with holy fire,
   with splendour he is crowned.
   How awesome is the sight,
   our radiant King of light!
   Be still, for the glory of the Lord
   is shining all around.

3. Be still, for the power of the Lord
   is moving in this place;
   he comes to cleanse and heal,
   to minister his grace.
   No work too hard for him,
   in faith receive from him.
   Be still, for the power of the Lord
   is moving in this place.

© 1986 Kingsway's Thankyou Music

34 Alan J. Price

1. Be the centre of my life, Lord Jesus,
   be the centre of life, I pray;
   be my Saviour to forgive me,
   be my friend to be with me,
   be the centre of my life today!

2. Let the power of your presence, Lord Jesus,
   from the centre of my life shine through;
   oh, let everybody know it,
   I really want to show it,
   that the centre of my life is you!

© 1990 Daybreak Music Ltd.

35 Bob Gillman

Bind us together, Lord,
bind us together,
with cords that cannot be broken.
Bind us together, Lord,
bind us together, Lord,
bind us together in love.

Continued overleaf

1. There is only one God,
   there is only one King.
   There is only one Body,
   that is why we sing:

   Bind us together, Lord,
   bind us together,
   with cords that cannot be broken.
   Bind us together, Lord,
   bind us together, Lord,
   bind us together in love.

2. Fit for the glory of God,
   purchased by his precious Blood,
   born with the right to be free:
   Jesus the victory has won.

3. We are the family of God,
   we are his promise divine,
   we are his chosen desire,
   we are the glorious new wine.

36 Kevin Mayhew

1. Blessed are my people, says the Lord.
   Blessed are my people, says the Lord.

   Come to me, friends of mine,
   come share my life divine,
   come to the banquet of the Lord.

2. Blessed are the lonely, says the Lord.
   Blessed are the lonely, says the Lord.

3. Blessed are the humble, says the Lord.
   Blessed are the humble, says the Lord.

4. Blessed are the downcast, says the Lord.
   Blessed are the downcast, says the Lord.

5. Blessed are the gentle, says the Lord.
   Blessed are the gentle, says the Lord.

6. Blessed are the hungry, says the Lord.
   Blessed are the hungry, says the Lord.

37 Hubert J. Richards

Blessed be God for ever, Amen,
blessed be God for ever, Amen,
blessed be God for ever, Amen.

1. Come, sing a new song to the Lord;
   Come, sing to the Lord, all the earth,
   and ring out your praises to God.

2. Come, tell of all his wondrous deeds,
   come, thank him for all he has done,
   and offer your gifts to the Lord.

3. Let all creation shout for joy;
   come, worship the Lord in his house,
   the Lord who made heaven and earth.

38 Taizé Community

Bless the Lord, my soul,
and bless God's holy name.
Bless the Lord, my soul,
who leads me into life.

39 from Psalm 103:1

Bless the Lord, O my soul;
bless the Lord, O my soul;
and all that is within me
bless God's holy name.

40 Aniceto Nazareth

1. Blest are you, Lord, God of all creation,
   thanks to your goodness this bread we offer:
   fruit of the earth, work of our hands,
   it will become the bread of life.

   Blessed be God! Blessed be God!
   Blessed be God for ever! Amen!
   Blessed be God! Blessed be God!
   Blessed be God for ever! Amen!

2. Blest are you, Lord, God of all creation,
   thanks to your goodness this wine we offer:
   fruit of the earth, work of our hands,
   it will become the cup of life.

41 Christopher Walker

Bread we bring to the God of love,
as an offering at his table laid,
bread of the earth, work of our hands.
Wine we bring to the God of love,
as an offering at his table laid,
fruit of the vine, work of our hands.

1. Lord, we bring you our doubt:
   for not trusting you,
   for not hearing you,
   in your mercy forgive.
   When we've gone astray
   from your gentle way,
   in your mercy forgive.

2. Lord, we bring you our strength:
   in the work we do
   may we follow you
   to the praise of your name.
   Father, make us strong,
   though the work be long,
   to the praise of your name.

3. Lord, we bring you our faith:
   through the gift of prayer
   may we learn to share
   in the love you have given;
   make us steadfast
   till we come, at last,
   to your kingdom in heaven.

42 Richard Gillard

1. Brother, sister, let me serve you,
   let me be as Christ to you;
   pray that I may have the grace to
   let you be my servant, too.

2. We are pilgrims on a journey,
   fellow trav'lers on the road;
   we are here to help each other
   walk the mile and bear the load.

3. I will hold the Christlight for you
   in the night-time of your fear;
   I will hold my hand out to you,
   speak the peace you long to hear.

4. I will weep when you are weeping;
   when you laugh, I'll laugh with you.
   I will share your joy and sorrow,
   till we've seen this journey through.

5. When we sing to God in heaven,
   we shall find such harmony,
   born of all we've known together
   of Christ's love and agony.

6. Brother, sister, let me serve you,
   let me be as Christ to you;
   pray that I may have the grace to
   let you be my servant, too.

43 Graham Jeffery

1. Build, build your Church, dear Lord;
   each soul's a living stone,
   cemented by your saving grace
   into its proper place.

   So build your Church,
   build your Church,
   each soul's a living stone.
   So build your Church,
   build your Church,
   each soul's a living stone.

2. Build, build your Church, dear Lord;
   you work with nails and wood,
   well used to fixing things in place
   with carefulness and grace.

3. Build, build your Church, dear Lord;
   though stones on earth seem few,
   let those whose lives are falling down
   be lifted up in you.

4. Build, build your Church, dear Lord;
   the door leave open wide,
   and all the people of the world
   will find their place inside.

44 Susan Sayers

1. Caterpillar, caterpillar, munching, munching,
   ate through a leaf or two,
   for caterpillar, caterpillar, munching, munching,
   didn't have a lot to do.
   But the leaves were very tasty,
   and there seemed a lot to spare,
   so caterpillar, caterpillar went on munching,
   munching everywhere.

2. Caterpillar, caterpillar, feeling sleepy,
   fixed up a silken bed.
   Then caterpillar, caterpillar climbed inside
   and covered up his sleepy head.
   In the dark he slept and rested
   as the days and nights went by,
   till on a sunny morning when the silk bed burst,
   he was a butterfly!

3. Butterfly, oh butterfly, a-flitt'ring, flutt'ring;
   oh what a sight to see.
   And as the lovely butterfly was flutt'ring by,
   I heard him sing a song to me:
   'Oh I never knew God could do
   such a wondrous thing for me;
   for he took me as a caterpillar and he made
   a butterfly of me.'

45 Eddie Espinosa

Change my heart, O God,
make it ever true,
change my heart, O God,
may I be like you.

You are the potter, I am the clay,
mould me and make me,
this is what I pray.

46 Estelle White

1. 'Cheep!' said the sparrow on the chimney top,
   'All my feathers are known to God.'
   'Caw!' said the rook in a tree so tall,
   'I know that God gladly made us all.'

2. 'Coo!' said the gentle one, the grey-blue dove,
   'I can tell you that God is love.'
   High up above sang the lark in flight,
   'I know the Lord is my heart's delight.'

3. 'Chirp!' said the robin with his breast so red,
   'I don't work at all, yet I'm fed.'
   'Whoo!' called the owl in a leafy wood.
   'Our God is wonderful, wise and good.'

47 adapted from 'St Patrick's Breastplate' by James Quinn

1. Christ be beside me, Christ be before me,
   Christ be behind me, King of my heart.
   Christ be within me, Christ be below me,
   Christ be above me, never to part.

2. Christ on my right hand, Christ on my left hand,
   Christ all around me, shield in the strife.
   Christ in my sleeping, Christ in my sitting,
   Christ in my rising, light of my life.

Continued overleaf

3. Christ be in all hearts thinking about me.
   Christ be in all tongues telling of me.
   Christ be the vision in eyes that see me,
   in ears that hear me, Christ ever be.

48 Jimmy Owens

Clap your hands, all you people.
Shout to our God with a voice of triumph.
Clap your hands, all you people.
Shout to our God with a voice of praise!
Hosanna, hosanna.
Shout to our God with a voice of triumph.
Praise him, praise him.
Shout to our God with a voice of praise!

49 Jean Holloway

1. Clap your hands and sing this song, all together,
   tap your feet and sing along, all together.

2. Raise your hands up in the air, all together,
   God can reach you anywhere, all together.

3. Fold your arms across your chest, all together,
   in the arms of God you're blessed, all together.

4. Close your eyes and shut them tight, all together,
   God will keep you in his sight, all together.

5. Now sing softly, whisper low, all together,
   God will hear you even so, all together.

6. Sing out loud and strong and clear, all together,
   so that everyone can hear, all together.

7. Sing with harmony and joy, all together,
   God loves every girl and boy, all together.

50 Sue McClellan, John Paculabo and Keith Ryecroft

1. Colours of day dawn into the mind,
   the sun has come up, the night is behind.
   Go down in the city, into the street,
   and let's give the message to the people we meet.

   So light up the fire and let the flame burn,
   open the door, let Jesus return.
   Take seeds of his Spirit, let the fruit grow,
   tell the people of Jesus, let his love show.

2. Go through the park, on into the town;
   the sun still shines on; it never goes down.
   The light of the world is risen again;
   the people of darkness are needing a friend.

3. Open your eyes, look into the sky,
   the darkness has come, the sun came to die.
   The evening draws on, the sun disappears,
   but Jesus is living, his Spirit is near.

51 Unknown

1. Come and go with me to my Father's house,
   to my Father's house, to my Father's house.
   Come and go with me to my Father's house
   where there's joy, joy, joy.

2. It's not very far to my Father's house . . .

3. There is room for all in my Father's house . . .

4. Ev'rything is free in my Father's house . . .

5. Jesus is the way to my Father's house . . .

6. Jesus is the light in my Father's house . . .

Suggestions for further verses:

We will clap our hands . . .

There is liberty . . .

We will praise the Lord . . .

52 Margaret Rizza

Come, Holy Spirit, bring us light,
teach us, heal us, give us life.
Come, Lord, O let our hearts flow
with love and all that is true.

53 Unknown

1. Come into his presence, singing,
   'Alleluia, alleluia, alleluia.'
   (Repeat)

2. Come into his presence, singing,
   'Jesus is Lord, Jesus is Lord, Jesus is Lord.'
   (Repeat)

3. Come into his presence, singing,
   'Glory to God, glory to God, glory to God.'

54 Mike Anderson

Come, let us raise a joyful song to the Lord,
a shout of triumph!
Come, let us raise a joyful song to the Lord,
and give him thanks!

1. The furthest places on the earth
   are in his hands.
   He made them, and we sing his praise.

2. The seas and waters on the earth
   are in his hands.
   He made them, and we sing his praise.

3. The hills and valleys on the earth
   are in his hands.
   He made them, and we sing his praise.

4. All living creatures on the earth
   are in his hands.
   He made them, and we sing his praise.

Continued overleaf

5. And we his people on the earth
   are in his hands.
   He saved us, and we sing his praise.

   Come, let us raise a joyful song to the Lord,
   a shout of triumph!
   Come, let us raise a joyful song to the Lord,
   and give him thanks!

55 Kevin Mayhew

1. Come, Lord Jesus, come.
   Come, take my hands,
   take them for your work.
   Take them for your service, Lord.
   Take them for your glory, Lord.
   Come, Lord Jesus, come.
   Come, Lord Jesus, take my hands.

2. Come, Lord Jesus, come.
   Come, take my eyes,
   may they shine with joy.
   Take them for your service, Lord.
   Take them for your glory, Lord.
   Come, Lord Jesus, come.
   Come, Lord Jesus, take my eyes.

3. Come, Lord Jesus, come.
   Come, take my lips,
   may they speak your truth.
   Take them for your service, Lord.
   Take them for your glory, Lord.
   Come, Lord Jesus, come.
   Come, Lord Jesus, take my lips.

4. Come, Lord Jesus, come.
   Come, take my feet,
   may they walk your path.
   Take them for your service, Lord.
   Take them for your glory, Lord.
   Come, Lord Jesus, come.
   Come, Lord Jesus, take my feet.

5. Come, Lord Jesus, come.
   Come, take my heart,
   fill it with your love.
   Take it for your service, Lord.
   Take it for your glory, Lord.
   Come, Lord Jesus, come.
   Come, Lord Jesus, take my heart.

6. Come, Lord Jesus, come.
   Come, take my life,
   take it for your own.
   Take it for your service, Lord.
   Take it for your glory, Lord.
   Come, Lord Jesus, come.
   Come, Lord Jesus, take my life.

56 Patricia Morgan and Dave Bankhead

Come on and celebrate!
His gift of love we will celebrate –
the Son of God who loved us
and gave us life.
We'll shout your praise, O King:
you give us joy nothing else can bring;
we'll give to you our offering
in celebration praise.

Continued overleaf

Come on and celebrate, celebrate,
celebrate and sing,
celebrate and sing to the King!
Come on and celebrate, celebrate,
celebrate and sing,
celebrate and sing to the King!

57 Graham Kendrick

Come on, let's get up and go.
Let everyone know.
We've got a reason to shout and to sing,
'cause Jesus loves us
and that's a wonderful thing.

Go! go! go! go! get up and go.
Don't be sleepy or slow.
You, you, you, you know what to do.
Give your life to him.

Come on, let's get up and go.
Let everyone know.
We've got a reason to shout and to sing,
'cause Jesus loves us
and that's a wonderful thing.

58 Unknown

Dear child divine, sweet brother mine,
be with me all the day,
and when the light has turned to night
be with me still, I pray.
Where'er I be come down to me
and never go away.

59 Gerard Markland

Do not be afraid,
for I have redeemed you.
I have called you by name;
you are mine.

1. When you walk through the waters I'll be with you.
   You will never sink beneath the waves.

2. When the fear of loneliness is looming,
   then remember I am at your side.

3. You are mine, O my child, I am your Father,
   and I love you with a perfect love.

© 1978 Kevin Mayhew Ltd.

60 Sebastian Temple

Do not worry over what to eat,
what to wear or put upon your feet.
Trust and pray, go do your best today,
then leave it in the hands of the Lord,
leave it in the hands of the Lord.

1. The lilies of the field, they do not spin or weave,
   yet Solomon was not arrayed like one of these.
   The birds of the air, they do not sow or reap,
   but God tends to them like a shepherd tends his sheep.

2. The Lord will guide you in his hidden way,
   show you what to do and tell you what to say.
   When you pray for rain, go build a dam to store
   every drop of water you have asked him for.

Continued overleaf

3. The Lord knows all your needs before you ask.
   Only trust in him for he will do the task
   of bringing in your life whatever you must know.
   He'll lead you through the darkness wherever you
        must go.

   Do not worry over what to eat,
   what to wear or put upon your feet.
   Trust and pray, go do your best today,
   then leave it in the hands of the Lord,
   leave it in the hands of the Lord.

61 Karen Lafferty

Don't build your house on the sandy land,
don't build it too near the shore.
Well, it might look kind of nice,
but you'll have to build it twice,
oh, you'll have to build your house once more.
You'd better build your house upon a rock,
make a good foundation on a solid spot.
Oh, the storms may come and go
but the peace of God you will know.

62 Bev Gammon

Lines in ordinary type are sung by the leader; those in
bold type by everybody.

Do what you know is right.
Do what you know is right.
Do what you know is good.

**Do what is good.
If no one else does it, don't be afraid.
Jesus says, 'I am with you always.'**

63 Michael Forster

1. Do you ever wish you could fly like a bird,
   or burrow like a worm? Well, how absurd!
   Think of all the things that you can do
   and just be glad God made you 'you'!

2. Do you ever wish you could swim like a duck?
   Unless your feet are webbed you're out of luck!
   Think of all the things that you can do
   and just be glad God made you 'you'!

3. Do you ever wish you could run like a hare?
   Well, wishing it won't get you anywhere!
   Think of all the things that you can do
   and just be glad God made you 'you'!

4. Do you ever wish you could hang like a bat?
   There's really not a lot of fun in that!
   Think of all the things that you can do
   and just be glad God made you 'you'!

5. Do you ever wish – well, that's really enough!
   To wish away your life is silly stuff!
   Think of all the things that you can do
   and just be glad God made you 'you'!

64 Michael Forster

Each of us is a living stone,
no one needs to stand alone,
joined to other living stones,
we're building the temple of God.

1. We're building, we're building the temple of God
       on earth,
   but it needs no walls or steeple,
   for we're making a house of greater worth,
   we're building it with people!

2. The stone that, the stone that the builders once
       cast aside
   has been made the firm foundation,
   and the carpenter who was crucified
   now offers us salvation.

65 Scripture

Eat this bread, drink this cup,
come to him and never be hungry.
Eat this bread, drink this cup,
trust in him and you will not thirst.

66 Peter Watcyn-Jones

1. Every bird, every tree
   helps me know, helps me see,
   helps me feel God
   is love and love's around.
   From each river painted blue
   to the early morning dew
   this is love, God is love, love's around.

2. Every prayer, every song
   makes me feel I belong
   to a world filled
   with love that's all around.
   From each daybreak to each night,
   out of darkness comes the light,
   this is love, God is love, love's around.

3. Every mountain, every stream,
   every flower, every dream
   comes from God,
   God is love and love's around.
   From the ever-changing sky
   to a new-born baby's cry,
   this is love, God is love, love's around.

67 Frank Andersen

1. Father, in my life I see
   you are God who walks with me.
   You hold my life in your hands:
   close beside you I will stand.
   I give all my life to you:
   help me, Father, to be true.

2. Jesus, in my life I see
   you are God who walks with me.
   You hold my life in your hands:
   close beside you I will stand.
   I give all my life to you:
   help me, Jesus, to be true.

Continued overleaf

3. Spirit, in my life I see
   you are God who walks with me.
   You hold my life in your hands:
   close beside you I will stand.
   I give all my life to you:
   help me, Spirit, to be true.

68 Jenny Hewer

1. Father, I place into your hands
   the things that I can't do.
   Father, I place into your hands
   the times that I've been through.
   Father, I place into your hands
   the way that I should go,
   for I know I always can trust you.

2. Father, I place into your hands
   my friends and family.
   Father, I place into your hands
   the things that trouble me.
   Father, I place into your hands
   the person I would be,
   for I know I always can trust you.

3. Father, we love to seek your face,
   we love to hear your voice.
   Father, we love to sing your praise
   and in your name rejoice.
   Father, we love to walk with you
   and in your presence rest,
   for we know we always can trust you.

4. Father, I want to be with you
   and do the things you do.
   Father, I want to speak the words
   that you are speaking too.
   Father, I want to love the ones
   that you will draw to you,
   for I know that I am one with you.

69 Terrye Coelho

1. Father, we adore you,
   lay our lives before you.
   How we love you!

2. Jesus, we adore you . . .

3. Spirit, we adore you . . .

70 Robin Mann

*Father welcomes all his children
to his fam'ly through his Son.
Father giving his salvation,
life for ever has been won.*

1. Little children, come to me,
   for my kingdom is of these.
   Love and new life have I to give,
   pardon for your sin.

Continued overleaf

2. In the water, in the word,
   in his promise, be assured:
   all who believe and are baptised
   shall be born again.

   Father welcomes all his children
   to his fam'ly through his Son.
   Father giving his salvation,
   life for ever has been won.

3. Let us daily die to sin;
   let us daily rise with him –
   walk in the love of Christ our Lord,
   live in the peace of God.

© 1986 Kevin Mayhew Ltd.

71 Donna Adkins

1. Father, we love you,
   we praise you, we adore you,
   glorify your name in all the earth.
   Glorify your name, glorify your name,
   glorify your name in all the earth.

2. Jesus, we love you . . .

3. Spirit, we love you . . .

© 1976 Maranatha! Music/CopyCare

72 Susan Sayers

Father, we want to thank you
for your loving kindness;
and to show you we love you
we will play our music for you.

1. Rum, tum, ta-rum, tum, tum,
   we play our drums for you, Lord Jesus.
   Rum, tum, ta-rum, tum, tum,
   we play our drums for you.

2. Ring, ting, ta-ting, ting, ting,
   we play our triangles for Jesus.
   Ring, ting, ta-ting, ting, ting,
   we play them, Lord, for you.

3. La, la, la-la, la, la,
   we sing our praises for you, Jesus.
   La, la, la-la, la, la,
   we sing our praise for you.

73 Peter Allen

Feed us now, O Son of God,
as you fed them long ago.

1. The people came to hear you,
   the poor, the lame, the blind.
   They asked for food to save them,
   you fed them body and mind.

2. The ones who didn't listen,
   the rich, the safe, the sure,
   they didn't think they needed
   the off'ring of a cure.

3. It's hard for us to listen,
   things haven't changed at all.
   We've got the things we wanted;
   we don't want to hear your call.

Continued overleaf

4. Yet millions still have hunger,
   disease, no homes, and fear.
   We offer them so little,
   and it costs them very dear.

   Feed us now, O Son of God,
   as you fed them long ago.

5. So help us see the writing,
   written clear upon the wall:
   he who doesn't feed his neighbour
   will get no food at all.

74 Susan Sayers

1. Fishes of the ocean and the birds of the air,
   they all declare the wonderful works of God
   who has created everything everywhere;
   let the whole earth sing of his love!

2. Apples in the orchard and the corn in the field,
   the plants all yield their fruit in due season,
   so the generosity of God is revealed;
   let the whole earth sing of his love!

3. Energy and colour from the sun with its light,
   the moon by night; the patterns of the stars
   all winking in the darkness on a frosty cold night;
   let the whole earth sing of his love!

4. Muddy hippopotamus and dainty gazelle,
   the mice as well, are all of his making,
   furry ones and hairy ones and some with a shell;
   let the whole earth sing of his love!

5. All that we can hear and everything we can see,
   including me, we all of us spring from God
   who cares for everybody unendingly;
   let the whole earth sing of his love!

75 Michael Cockett

Follow me, follow me,
leave your home and family,
leave your fishing nets and boats upon the shore.
Leave the seeds that you have sown,
leave the crops that you've grown,
leave the people you have known and follow me.

1. The foxes have their holes
   and the swallows have their nests,
   but the Son of Man has no place to lie down.
   I do not offer comfort,
   I do not offer wealth,
   but in me will true happiness be found.

2. If you would follow me,
   you must leave old ways behind.
   You must take my cross and follow on my path.
   You may be far from loved ones,
   you may be far from home,
   but my Father will welcome you at last.

3. Although I go away
   you will never be alone,
   for the Spirit will be there to comfort you.
   Though all of you may scatter,
   each follow their own path,
   still the Spirit of love will lead you home.

76 Graham Jeffery

1. Forward in faith,
   forward in Christ,
   we are travelling onward;
   forward in faith,
   forward in Christ,
   we are trav'ling on.

   Onward, onward,
   we are trav'ling on,
   onward, onward,
   we are trav'ling on.

2. Jesus is Lord,
   Jesus is Lord,
   we are travelling onward;
   Jesus is Lord,
   Jesus is Lord,
   We are trav'ling on.

3. He is our King,
   he is our King,
   we are travelling onward;
   he is our King, he is our King,
   we are trav'ling on.

77 Damian Lundy

Freedom for my people!
Freedom for my people!
Call them to liberty! Alleluia! Healing!
Liberation for a new creation!
Set all my people free!

1. Moses was the man I called to liberty;
   sent him back to Pharaoh's court to set my people free.
   He led all my people out to liberty,
   calling them to leave that land of their slavery.

2. Through the desert they were led to liberty;
   with the manna they were fed so they could be free.
   And I gave my law to them for liberty,
   so that they might live in peace and in unity.

3. Oh, when will my people know how to be free?
   All my prophets tried to show: the people would not see.
   So I gave my only Son, precious to me;
   on the cross he hung in pain for your liberty.

4. Jesus rose on Easter Day to liberty.
   He will never go away – he will set you free!
   Never will he die again! He is with me,
   and we have begun our reign with his victory!

   Gloria! Alleluia!
   Gloria! Alleluia!
   Sing of his victory! Alleluia!
   Gloria! Alleluia!
   Gloria! Alleluia!
   Set all my people free!

5. I'm your God and you are mine: now you are free!
   Eat my bread and drink my wine! Come and
      follow me!
   You will know my Spirit's love and you will see
   power coming from above to set all people free!

Refrain followed by second refrain: *Gloria! Alleluia!*

78 David Morstad

Friends, all gather here in a circle.
It has no beginning and it has no end.
Face to face, we all have a place
in God's own circle of friends.
Hey there, (name)!
How do you do?
Who's that friend sitting close to you?
Thank the Lord, for (name) has a place in the circle, too.
Take a look around.
Find someone near.
Take him/her by the hand,
say, 'Glad you're here.'
We're together and when we've gone,
God's love like a circle rolls on and on and on.

79 Graham Kendrick

1. From heav'n you came, helpless babe,
   entered our world, your glory veiled;
   not to be served but to serve,
   and give your life that we might live.

   This is our God, the Servant King,
   he calls us now to follow him,
   to bring our lives as a daily offering
   of worship to the Servant King.

2. There in the garden of tears,
   my heavy load he chose to bear;
   his heart with sorrow was torn,
   'Yet not my will, but yours,' he said.

3. Come, see his hands and his feet,
   the scars that speak of sacrifice,
   hands that flung stars into space
   to cruel nails surrendered.

4. So let us learn how to serve,
   and in our lives enthrone him;
   each other's needs to prefer,
   for it is Christ we're serving.

80 Jean Holloway

Gather around for the table is spread,
welcome the food and rest!
Wide is our circle, with Christ at the head,
he is the honoured guest.
Learn of his love, grow in his grace,
pray for the peace he gives;
here at this meal, here in this place,
know that his spirit lives!
Once he was known in the breaking of bread,
shared with a chosen few;
multitudes gathered and by him were fed,
so will he feed us too.

81 Christine McCann

1. Gifts of bread and wine, gifts we've offered,
   fruits of labour, fruits of love;
   taken, offered, sanctified,
   blessed and broken; words of one who died:

   'Take my body, take my saving blood.'
   Gifts of bread and wine: Christ our Lord.

2. Christ our Saviour, living presence here,
   as he promised while on earth:
   'I am with you for all time,
   I am with you in this bread and wine.'

3. Through the Father, with the Spirit,
   one in union with the Son,
   for God's people, joined in prayer,
   faith is strengthened by the food we share.

© 1978 Kevin Mayhew Ltd.

82 Traditional

1. Give me joy in my heart, keep me praising,
   give me joy in my heart, I pray.
   Give me joy in my heart, keep me praising,
   keep me praising till the end of day.

   Sing hosanna! Sing hosanna!
   Sing hosanna to the King of kings!
   Sing hosanna! Sing hosanna!
   Sing hosanna to the King!

2. Give me peace in my heart, keep me resting . . .

3. Give me love in my heart, keep me serving . . .

4. Give me oil in my lamp, keep me burning . . .

83 Estelle White

1. Give me peace, O Lord, I pray,
   in my work and in my play;
   and inside my heart and mind,
   Lord, give me peace.

2. Give peace to the world, I pray,
   let all quarrels cease today.
   May we spread your light and love.
   Lord, give us peace.

84 Janet Morgan

Give thanks to the Lord for he is good.
Give thanks to the Lord for ever.
Give thanks to the Lord for he is good.

1. When you jump out of bed
   and you touch your toes,
   when you brush your teeth
   and put on your clothes:

2. When you eat your dinner
   and you're all full up,
   when your mum says (name),
   and you help wash up:

3. When you stretch up high
   and you touch the ground,
   when you stretch out wide
   and you turn around:

Continued overleaf

4. When you click your fingers
   and you stamp your feet,
   when you clap your hands
   and you slap your knees:

   Give thanks to the Lord for he is good.
   Give thanks to the Lord for ever.
   Give thanks to the Lord for he is good.
   Give thanks to the Lord. Amen.

85 Henry Smith

Give thanks with a grateful heart,
give thanks to the Holy One;
give thanks because he's given
Jesus Christ, his Son.
Give thanks with a grateful heart,
give thanks to the Holy One;
give thanks because he's given
Jesus Christ, his Son.

And now, let the weak say, 'I am strong',
let the poor say, 'I am rich',
because of what the Lord has done for us.
And now, let the weak say, 'I am strong',
let the poor say, 'I am rich',
because of what the Lord has done for us.

Give thanks.

86 Sebastian Temple

1. Glorious God, King of creation,
   we praise you, we bless you,
   we worship you in song.
   Glorious God, in adoration,
   at your feet we belong.

   Lord of life, Father almighty,
   Lord of hearts, Christ the King.
   Lord of love, Holy Spirit,
   to whom we homage bring.

2. Glorious God, magnificent, holy,
   we love you, adore you,
   and come to you in prayer.
   Glorious God, mighty, eternal,
   we sing your praise everywhere.

87 Thomas Ken

Glory to you, my God, this night,
for all the blessings of the light;
keep me, O keep me, King of kings,
beneath your own almighty wings.

88 Caroline Somerville

1. God almighty set a rainbow
   arching in the sky above,
   and his people understand it
   as a signal of his love.

Continued overleaf

Thank you, Father, thank you, Father,
thank you, Father, for your care,
for your warm and loving kindness
to your people everywhere.

2. Clouds will gather, storms come streaming
   on the darkened earth below –
   too much sunshine makes a desert,
   without rain no seed can grow.

3. Through the stormcloud shines your rainbow,
   through the dark earth springs the wheat.
   In the future waits your harvest
   and the food for all to eat.

4. God almighty, you have promised
   after rain the sun will show;
   bless the seeds and bless the harvest.
   Give us grace to help us grow.

89 Michael Forster

1. God cares for all creation
   as a shepherd for the sheep,
   he is everything
   the world can ever need.
   In green and peaceful places,
   and where gentle waters flow,
   we'll follow him wherever he may lead.

   'I'm the shepherd who cares for the sheep,' he says,
   'and my promise you know I will keep,' he says,
   'though the path may be rocky and steep,' he says,
   'I will love you and lead you for ever.'

2. Yes, even in the darkness,
   there's no need to be afraid
   in the shadow and mystery of death;
   for God is always with us,
   giving confidence and hope,
   his spirit calms the trembling of our breath.

3. Though others may assail us,
   he assures us of his love,
   and prepares a feast so everyone will know.
   He comforts us with kindness
   like a sweetly scented oil,
   while gladness and contentment overflow.

4. We know his love and goodness
   will be with us all our days,
   as we go in faith where he has gone before.
   His love will never falter,
   nor his ancient promise fail,
   and we shall live with him for evermore.

90 Carol Owens

1. God forgave my sin in Jesus' name,
   I've been born again in Jesus' name;
   and in Jesus' name I come to you
   to share his love as he told me to.

   He said, 'Freely, freely you have received;
   freely, freely give.
   Go in my name, and because you believe,
   others will know that I live.'

Continued overleaf

2. All pow'r is given in Jesus' name,
   in earth and heav'n in Jesus' name;
   and in Jesus' name I come to you
   to share his pow'r as he told me to.

   He said, 'Freely, freely you have received;
   freely, freely give.
   Go in my name, and because you believe,
   others will know that I live.'

3. God gives us life in Jesus' name,
   he lives in us in Jesus' name;
   and in Jesus' name I come to you
   to share his peace as he told me to.

91 Sr Miriam Therese Winter

1. God gives his people strength.
   If we believe in his way
   he's swift to repay
   all those who bear the burden of the day.
   God gives his people strength.

2. God gives his people hope.
   If we but trust in his word
   our prayers are always heard.
   He warmly welcomes anyone who's erred.
   God gives his people hope.

3. God gives his people love.
   If we but open wide our heart
   he's sure to do his part.
   He's always the first to make a start.
   God gives his people love.

4. God gives his people peace.
   When sorrow fills us to the brim
   and courage grows dim
   he lays to rest our restlessness in him.
   God gives his people peace.

92 Bernadette Farrell

1. God has chosen me, God has chosen me
   to bring good news to the poor.
   God has chosen me, God has chosen me
   to bring new sight to those searching for light:
   God has chosen me, chosen me:

   and to tell the world that God's kingdom is near,
   to remove oppression and break down fear,
   yes, God's time is near, God's time is near,
   God's time is near, God's time is near.

2. God has chosen me, God has chosen me
   to set alight a new fire.
   God has chosen me, God has chosen me
   to bring to birth a new kingdom on earth:
   God has chosen me, chosen me:

3. God is calling me, God is calling me
   in all whose cry is unheard.
   God is calling me, God is calling me
   to raise up the voice with no power or choice:
   God is calling me, calling me:

1. God is love, and the ones who live in love
live in God, and God lives in them.
God is love, and the ones who live in love
live in God, and God lives in them.
And we have come to know and have believed
the love which God has for us.
God is love, and the ones who live in love
live in God, and God lives in them.

2. God is hope, and the ones who live in hope
live in God, and God lives in them.
God is hope, and the ones who live in hope
live in God, and God lives in them.
And we have come to know and have believed
the love which God has for us.
God is hope, and the ones who live in hope
live in God, and God lives in them.

3. God is peace, and the ones who live in peace
live in God, and God lives in them.
God is peace, and the ones who live in peace
live in God, and God lives in them.
And we have come to know and have believed
the love which God has for us.
God is peace, and the ones who live in peace
live in God, and God lives in them.

4. God is joy, and the ones who live in joy
live in God, and God lives in them.
God is joy, and the ones who live in joy
live in God, and God lives in them.
And we have come to know and have believed
the love which God has for us.
God is joy, and the ones who live in joy
live in God, and God lives in them.

94 Kathleen Middleton

1. God our Father gave us life,
   he keeps us in his care;
   help us care for others too:
   Lord, hear our prayer;
   Lord, hear our prayer.

2. When we're frightened, hurt or tired,
   there's always someone there.
   Make us thankful for their love:
   Lord, hear our prayer;
   Lord, hear our prayer.

3. All God's children need his love,
   a love that we can share.
   So, we pray for everyone:
   Lord, hear our prayer;
   Lord, hear our prayer.

95 Michael Forster

1. God sends a rainbow after the rain,
   colours of hope gleaming through pain;
   bright arcs of red and indigo light,
   making creation hopeful and bright.

   Colours of hope dance in the sun,
   while it yet rains the hope has begun;
   colours of hope shine through the rain,
   colours of love, nothing is vain.

Continued overleaf

2. When we are lonely, when we're afraid,
   though it seems dark, rainbows are made;
   even when life itself has to end,
   God is our rainbow, God is our friend.

   Colours of hope dance in the sun,
   while it yet rains the hope has begun;
   colours of hope shine through the rain,
   colours of love, nothing is vain.

3. Where people suffer pain or despair,
   God can be seen in those who care;
   even where war and hatred abound,
   rainbows of hope are still to be found.

4. People themselves like rainbows are made,
   colours of hope in us displayed;
   old ones and young ones, women and men,
   all can be part of love's great 'Amen'!

96 Ian D. Craig

1. God's love is deeper than the deepest ocean,
   God's love is wider than the widest sea,
   God's love is higher than the highest mountain,
   deeper, wider, higher is God's love to me.

2. God's grace is deeper than the deepest ocean,
   God's grace is wider than the widest sea,
   God's grace is higher than the highest mountain,
   deeper, wider, higher is God's grace to me.

3. God's joy is deeper than the deepest ocean,
   God's joy is wider than the widest sea,
   God's joy is higher than the highest mountain,
   deeper, wider, higher is God's joy to me.

4. God's peace is deeper than the deepest ocean,
   God's peace is wider than the widest sea,
   God's peace is higher than the highest mountain,
   deeper, wider, higher is God's peace to me.
   Deeper, wider, higher,
   deeper, wider, higher,
   deeper, wider, higher is God to me.

97 Alan Dale and Hubert J. Richards

1. God's Spirit is in my heart.
   He has called me and set me apart.
   This is what I have to do,
   what I have to do.

   He sent me to give the Good News to the poor
   tell pris'ners that they are pris'ners no more,
   tell blind people that they can see,
   and set the downtrodden free,
   and go tell everyone
   the news that the kingdom of God has come,
   and go tell everyone
   the news that God's kingdom has come.

2. Just as the Father sent me,
   so I'm sending you out to be
   my witnesses throughout the world,
   the whole of the world.

Continued overleaf

3. Don't carry a load in your pack,
   you don't need two shirts on your back.
   A workman can earn his own keep,
   can earn his own keep.

   He sent me to give the Good News to the poor
   tell pris'ners that they are pris'ners no more,
   tell blind people that they can see,
   and set the downtrodden free,
   and go tell everyone
   the news that the kingdom of God has come,
   and go tell everyone
   the news that God's kingdom has come.

4. Don't worry what you have to say,
   don't worry because on that day
   God's Spirit will speak in your heart,
   will speak in your heart.

© 1982 Kevin Mayhew Ltd.

98 Michael Forster

1. God turned darkness into light,
   separated day from night,
   looked upon it with delight,
   and declared that it was good.

   God was pleased with everything,
   God was pleased with everything,
   God was pleased with everything,
   and declared that it was good.

2. God divided land and sea,
   filled the world with plants and trees,
   all so beautiful to see,
   and declared that it was good.

3. God made animals galore,
   fishes, birds and dinosaurs,
   heard the splashes, songs and roars,
   and declared that it was good.

4. God made people last of all,
   black and white, and short and tall,
   male and female, large and small,
   and declared that it was good.

99 Michael Forster

1. Goliath was big and Goliath was strong,
   his sword was sharp and his spear was long;
   he bragged and boasted but he was wrong:
   biggest isn't always best!

   Biggest isn't always best!
   Biggest isn't always best!
   God told David, 'Don't be afraid,
   biggest isn't always best!'

2. A shepherd boy had a stone and sling;
   he won the battle and pleased the King!
   Then all the people began to sing:
   'Biggest isn't always best!'

3. So creatures made in a smaller size,
   like tiny sparrows and butterflies,
   are greater than we may realise:
   biggest isn't always best!

100 Marie Lydia Pereira

1. Go, the Mass is ended,
   children of the Lord.
   Take his Word to others
   as you've heard it spoken to you.
   Go, the Mass is ended,
   go and tell the world
   the Lord is good, the Lord is kind,
   and he loves everyone.

2. Go, the Mass is ended,
   take his love to all.
   Gladden all who meet you,
   fill their hearts with hope and courage.
   Go, the Mass is ended,
   fill the world with love,
   and give to all what you've received
   – the peace and joy of Christ.

3. Go, the Mass is ended,
   strengthened in the Lord,
   lighten every burden,
   spread the joy of Christ around you.
   Go, the Mass is ended,
   take his peace to all.
   This day is yours to change the world
   – to make God known and loved.

101 Susan Sayers

1. Go wand'ring in the sun,
   let it warm you through.
   That's how warm and comforting
   God's love can be for you.

2. Just watch a feather fall,
   lay it on your cheek.
   Jesus is as gentle
   with the frightened and the weak.

3. Enjoy the drops of rain,
   sparkling as they fall.
   Jesus is as gen'rous
   with his blessings to us all.

4. Well, can you hold the sea,
   make a living flow'r?
   Neither can we understand
   the greatness of his pow'r.

5. Yet run against the wind –
   very soon you'll see –
   just as strong and free
   is Jesus' love for you and me.

102 Aniceto Nazareth

   Great indeed are your works, O Lord,
   now and evermore!
   Great indeed are your works, O Lord,
   now and evermore!

1. The universe, night and day,
   tells of all your wonders.
   You are our life and our light:
   we shall praise you always.

2. You are the path which we tread,
   you will lead us onward.
   From every corner of earth
   all the nations gather.

Continued overleaf

3. You lead them all by the hand
   to the heav'nly kingdom.
   Then, at the end of all time,
   you will come in glory.

   Great indeed are your works, O Lord,
   now and evermore!
   Great indeed are your works, O Lord,
   now and evermore!

103 Scripture

Hail, Mary, full of grace,
the Lord is with thee.
Blessed art thou among women,
and blessed is the fruit of thy womb, Jesus.
Holy Mary, mother of God,
pray for us sinners, now
and at the hour of our death. Amen.

104 Traditional

Halle, halle, hallelujah!
Halle, halle, hallelujah!
Halle, halle, hallelujah!
Hallelujah, hallelujah!

105 Unknown

Hallelu, hallelu, hallelu, hallelujah;
we'll praise the Lord!
Hallelu, hallelu, hallelu, hallelujah;
we'll praise the Lord!

We'll praise the Lord, hallelujah!
We'll praise the Lord, hallelujah!
We'll praise the Lord, hallelujah!
We'll praise the Lord!

106 Richard Hubbard

1. Hang on, stand still,
   stay put, hold tight;
   wait for the Spirit of God.
   Don't push, don't shove,
   don't move, that's right,
   just wait for the Spirit of God.
   (Repeat)

   For you will receive the power of God,
   you will receive the power of God,
   you will receive the power of God
   when the Holy Spirit is upon you.

2. Let go, launch out,
   press on, don't fight;
   be filled with the Spirit of God.
   Move on, make way,
   step out, that's right;
   be filled with the Spirit of God.
   (Repeat)

   For you have received the power of God,
   you have received the power of God,
   you have received the power of God,
   now the Holy Spirit lives within you.

107 Christian Strover

1. Have you heard the raindrops drumming on the
   rooftops?
   Have you heard the raindrops dripping on the ground?
   Have you heard the raindrops splashing in the streams
   and running to the rivers all around?

   There's water, water of life,
   Jesus gives us the water of life;
   there's water, water of life,
   Jesus gives us the water of life.

2. There's a busy worker digging in the desert,
   digging with a spade that flashes in the sun;
   soon there will be water rising in the well-shaft,
   spilling from the bucket as it comes.

3. Nobody can live who hasn't any water,
   when the land is dry, then nothing much grows;
   Jesus gives us life if we drink the living water,
   sing it so that everybody knows.

108 Eileen Russell

Hear what God says to you and everyone,
hear what God says to you in his word:
'I have loved you with an everlasting love,
I have loved you with an everlasting love.'

109 Alan Pinnock

1. He gave me eyes so I could see
the wonders of the world.
Without my eyes I could not see
the other boys and girls.
He gave me ears so I could hear
the wind and rain and sea.
I've got to tell it to the world:
he made me.

2. He gave me lips so I could speak
and say what's in my mind.
Without my lips I could not speak
a single word or line.
He made my mind so I could think,
and choose what I should be.
I've got to tell it to the world:
he made me.

110 Unknown

He is the King of kings,
he is the Lord of lords,
his name is Jesus, Jesus, Jesus, Jesus,
O, he is the King.

111 Traditional

1. He's got the whole world in his hand.
He's got the whole world in his hand.
He's got the whole world in his hand.
He's got the whole world in his hand.

Continued overleaf

2. He's got you and me, brother, in his hand. (3)
   He's got the whole world in his hand.

3. He's got you and me, sister, in his hand. (3)
   He's got the whole world in his hand.

4. He's got the tiny little baby in his hand.
   He's got the whole world in his hand.

5. He's got everybody here in his hand. (3)
   He's got the whole world in his hand.

112 S. E. Cox

He's the same today as yesterday,
my great unchanging friend;
he's the same today as yesterday,
just the same unto the end.
By his mighty pow'r he holds me,
in his arms of love enfolds me;
he's the same today as yesterday,
my great unchanging friend.

113 Orien Johnson

Hey, now, everybody sing,
everybody sing to the Lord our God!
Hey, now, everybody sing,
everybody sing to the Lord our God!

Everybody join in a song of praise,
come and sing along with me!
Glory, alleluia,
glory, alleluia,
I'm so glad I'm free!

Hey, now, everybody sing,
everybody sing to the Lord our God!
Hey, now, everybody sing,
everybody sing to the Lord our God!
Everybody sing, everybody sing,
everybody sing to the Lord our God!
Everybody sing, everybody sing,
everybody sing to the Lord our God!
Everybody sing!

114 Adapted by Kevin Mayhew from the Aaronic Blessing

Holy God, we place ourselves into your hands.
Bless us and care for us,
be gracious and loving to us;
look kindly upon us, and give us peace.

115 Jimmy Owens

1. Holy, holy, holy, holy.
   Holy, holy, holy Lord God almighty;
   and we lift our hearts before you as a token of
       our love,
   holy, holy, holy, holy.

2. Gracious Father, gracious Father,
   we are glad to be your children, gracious Father;
   and we lift our heads before you as a token of
       our love,
   gracious Father, gracious Father.

Continued overleaf

3. Risen Jesus, risen Jesus,
   we are glad you have redeemed us, risen Jesus;
   and we lift our hands before you as a token of
      our love,
   risen Jesus, risen Jesus.

4. Holy Spirit, Holy Spirit,
   come and fill our hearts anew, Holy Spirit;
   and we lift our voice before you as a token of
      our love,
   Holy Spirit, Holy Spirit.

5. Hallelujah, hallelujah,
   Hallelujah, hallelujah, hallelujah;
   and we lift our hearts before you as a token of
      our love,
   hallelujah, hallelujah.

116 Unknown

1. Holy, holy, holy is the Lord,
   holy is the Lord God almighty.
   Holy, holy, holy is the Lord,
   holy is the Lord God almighty:
   who was, and is, and is to come;
   holy, holy, holy is the Lord.

2. Jesus, Jesus, Jesus is the Lord,
   Jesus is the Lord God almighty.
   Jesus, Jesus, Jesus is the Lord,
   Jesus is the Lord God almighty:
   who was, and is, and is to come;
   Jesus, Jesus, Jesus is the Lord.

3. Worthy, worthy, worthy is the Lord,
   worthy is the Lord God almighty.
   Worthy, worthy, worthy is the Lord,
   worthy is the Lord God almighty:
   who was, and is, and is to come;
   worthy, worthy, worthy is the Lord.

4. Glory, glory, glory to the Lord,
   glory to the Lord God almighty.
   Glory, glory, glory to the Lord,
   glory to the Lord God almighty:
   who was, and is, and is to come;
   glory, glory, glory to the Lord.

117 Damian Lundy

1. Holy Mary, you were chosen
   by the Father, the God of life.
   Joyfully responding,
   you became a mother.
   Pray now for us and show a mother's love.

2. Holy Mary, you were chosen,
   called to carry the Son of God.
   Gratefully responding,
   you became his mother.
   Pray now for us and show a mother's love.

3. Holy Mary, you were chosen,
   so the Spirit could work in you.
   Faithfully responding,
   you became God's mother.
   Pray now for us and show a mother's love.

Continued overleaf

4. Holy Mary, you were chosen:
   all God's children are blessed in you.
   Joyfully responding,
   you became our mother.
   Pray now for us and show a mother's love.

118 John Glynn

1. Holy Spirit of fire,
   flame everlasting, so bright and clear,
   speak this day in our hearts.
   Lighten our darkness and purge us of fear,
   Holy Spirit of fire.

   The wind can blow or be still,
   or water be parched by the sun.
   A fire can die into dust:
   But here the eternal Spirit of God
   tells us a new world's begun.

2. Holy Spirit of love,
   strong are the faithful who trust your power.
   Love who conquer our will,
   teach us the words of the gospel of peace,
   Holy Spirit of love.

3. Holy Spirit of God,
   flame everlasting so bright and clear,
   speak this day in our hearts.
   Lighten our darkness and purge us of fear,
   Holy Spirit of God.

119 Jean-Paul Lécot, trans. W. R. Lawrence

1. Holy virgin, by God's decree,
   you were called eternally;
   that he could give his Son to our race.
   Mary, we praise you, hail, full of grace.

   Ave, ave, ave, Maria.

2. By your faith and loving accord,
   as the handmaid of the Lord,
   you undertook God's plan to embrace.
   Mary, we thank you, hail, full of grace.

3. Joy to God you gave and expressed,
   of all women none more blessed,
   when in our world your Son took his place.
   Mary, we love you, hail, full of grace.

4. Refuge for your children so weak,
   sure protection all can seek.
   Problems of life you help us to face.
   Mary, we trust you, hail, full of grace.

5. To our needy world of today,
   love and beauty you portray,
   showing the path to Christ we must trace.
   Mary, our mother, hail, full of grace.

120 Hugh Mitchell

How did Moses cross the Red Sea?
How did Moses cross the Red Sea?
How did Moses cross the Red Sea?
How did he get across?
Did he swim? No! No!
Did he row? No! No!
Did he jump? No! No! No! No!
Did he drive? No! No!
Did he fly? No! No!
How did he get across?
God blew with his wind, puff, puff, puff, puff,
he blew just enough, 'nough, 'nough, 'nough, 'nough,
and through the sea he made a path,
that's how he got across.

121 Unknown

How great is our God,
how great is his name!
How great is our God,
for ever the same!

1. He rolled back the waters
   of the mighty Red Sea,
   and he said, 'I'll never leave you.
   Put your trust in me.'

2. He sent his Son, Jesus,
   to set us all free,
   and he said, 'I'll never leave you.
   Put your trust in me.'

3. He gave us his Spirit,
   and now we can see.
   And he said, 'I'll never leave you.
   Put your trust in me.'

122 Leonard E. Smith Jnr

1. How lovely on the mountains
   are the feet of him
   who brings good news, good news,
   proclaiming peace,
   announcing news of happiness:
   our God reigns, our God reigns.

   *Our God reigns, our God reigns,
   our God reigns, our God reigns.*

2. You watchmen, lift your voices
   joyfully as one,
   shout for your King, your King!
   See eye to eye,
   the Lord restoring Zion:
   our God reigns, our God reigns . . .

3. Waste places of Jerusalem,
   break forth with joy!
   We are redeemed, redeemed.
   The Lord has saved
   and comforted his people.
   Our God reigns, our God reigns . . .

4. Ends of the earth,
   see the salvation of our God!
   Jesus is Lord, is Lord!
   Before the nations
   he has bared his holy arm.
   Our God reigns, our God reigns . . .

123 David Konstant

1. I am the bread of life,
   You who come to me will never be hungry.
   I will raise you up.
   I will raise you up.
   I will raise you up to eternal life.
   I am the bread of life.

2. I am the spring of life.
   You who hope in me will never be thirsty.
   I will raise you up,
   I will raise you up,
   I will raise you up to eternal life.
   I am the spring of life.

3. I am the way of life.
   You who follow me will never be lonely.
   I will raise you up,
   I will raise you up,
   I will raise you up to eternal life.
   I am the way of life.

4. I am the truth of life.
   You who look for me will never seek blindly.
   I will raise you up,
   I will raise you up,
   I will raise you up to eternal life.
   I am the truth of life.

5. I am the life of life.
   You who die with me will never die vainly.
   I will raise you up,
   I will raise you up,
   I will raise you up to eternal life.
   I am the life of life.

124 Suzanne Toolan

1. I am the bread of life.
   You who come to me shall not hunger;
   and who believe in me shall not thirst.
   No one can come to me
   unless the Father beckons.

   And I will raise you up,
   and I will raise you up,
   and I will raise you up on the last day.

2. The bread that I will give
   is my flesh for the life of the world,
   and if you eat of this bread,
   you shall live for ever,
   you shall live for ever.

3. Unless you eat
   of the flesh of the Son of Man,
   and drink of his blood,
   and drink of his blood,
   you shall not have life within you.

4. I am the resurrection,
   I am the life.
   If you believe in me,
   even though you die,
   you shall live for ever.

5. Yes, Lord, I believe
   that you are the Christ,
   the Son of God,
   who has come
   into the world.

125 Sydney Carter

1. I come like a beggar with a gift in my hand,
   I come like a beggar with a gift in my hand.

   By the hungry I will feed you,
   by the poor I make you rich,
   by the broken I will mend you,
   tell me, which one is which?

2. I come like a prisoner to set you free,
   I come like a prisoner to set you free.

3. The need of another is the gift that I bring,
   the need of another is the gift that I bring.

4. I come like a beggar, what you do for my sake
   is the wine that I offer you, the bread that I break.

126 Sydney Carter

1. I danced in the morning when the world was begun,
   and I danced in the moon and the stars and the sun,
   and I came down from heaven and I danced on
       the earth,
   at Bethlehem I had my birth.

   Dance, then, wherever you may be,
   I am the Lord of the Dance, said he,
   and I'll lead you all, wherever you may be,
   and I'll lead you all in the dance, said he.

2. I danced for the scribe and the pharisee,
   but they would not dance and they wouldn't
      follow me.
   I danced for the fishermen, for James and John –
   they came with me and the dance went on.

3. I danced on the Sabbath and I cured the lame;
   the holy people said it was a shame.
   They whipped and they stripped and they hung me
      on high,
   and they left me there on a cross to die.

4. I danced on a Friday when the sky turned black –
   it's hard to dance with the devil on your back.
   They buried my body, and they thought I'd gone,
   but I am the dance, and I still go on.

5. They cut me down and I leapt up high;
   I am the life that'll never, never die;
   I'll live in you if you'll live in me –
   I am the Lord of the Dance, said he.

127 Susan Sayers

1. I feel spring in the air today,
   lots of flowers are on their way,
   bursting up to the light of day,
   for the earth is springing to life.

2. I feel spring in the air today,
   lambs are ready to frisk and play;
   nests are built as the tall trees sway,
   for the earth is springing to life.

Continued overleaf

3. I feel spring in the air today,
   Lord and Father, I want to say
   thanks for showing your love this way,
   for the earth is springing to life.

128 Damian Lundy

If I am lacking love,
then I am nothing, Lord.
On love I set my heart;
my joy and my reward.

1. Without love my words ring hollow,
   my intentions are disgraced,
   all my sacrifices empty,
   every hope and prayer misplaced.

2. Love is patient, love is kindly,
   never jealous, never proud;
   not conceited, nor ill-mannered,
   never selfish, never rude.

3. Love is gracious and forgiving,
   taking no delight in sin;
   love rejoices in the truth,
   will not lose heart, will not give in.

4. I know love is everlasting;
   other gifts will pass away.
   Only faith and hope and love
   will never die, will ever stay.

5. God is bountiful in giving;
   all his gifts are my desire,
   but I set my heart on love.
   May his love set my heart on fire!

129 Brian Howard

1. If I were a butterfly,
   I'd thank you, Lord, for giving me wings,
   and if I were a robin in a tree,
   I'd thank you, Lord, that I could sing,
   and if I were a fish in the sea,
   I'd wiggle my tail and I'd giggle with glee,
   but I just thank you, Father, for making me 'me'.

   For you gave me a heart,
   and you gave me a smile,
   you gave me Jesus
   and you made me your child,
   and I just thank you, Father,
   for making me 'me'.

2. If I were an elephant,
   I'd thank you, Lord, by raising my trunk,
   and if I were a kangaroo,
   you know I'd hop right up to you,
   and if I were an octopus,
   I'd thank you, Lord, for my fine looks,
   but I just thank you, Father,
   for making me 'me'.

Continued overleaf

3. If I were a wiggly worm,
   I'd thank you, Lord, that I could squirm,
   and if I were a billy goat,
   I'd thank you, Lord, for my strong throat,
   and if I were a fuzzy wuzzy bear,
   I'd thank you, Lord, for my fuzzy wuzzy hair,
   but I just thank you, Father,
   for making me 'me'.

   For you gave me a heart,
   and you gave me a smile,
   you gave me Jesus
   and you made me your child,
   and I just thank you, Father,
   for making me 'me'.

130 Susan Sayers

1. If I were an astronaut out in space,
   I'd watch the world spin by,
   a bright coloured marble lit up by the sun
   and set in an indigo sky.

   Ours to enjoy, ours to look after,
   oh what a wonderful world.

2. If I were a monkey, and treetop high,
   I'd see the fruits that grow,
   delicious and succulent, fragrant and sweet,
   on branches above and below.

3. If I were an octopus in the sea,
   the sun would filter through
   to dapple the corals and brighten the shells
   down deep in an ocean of blue.

131 Estelle White

1. I give my hands to do your work
   and, Jesus, Lord, I give them willingly.
   I give my feet to go your way
   and every step I shall take cheerfully.

   O, the joy of the Lord is my strength, my strength!
   O, the joy of the Lord is my help, my help!
   For the pow'r of his Spirit is in my soul
   and the joy of the Lord is my strength.

2. I give my eyes to see the world
   and everyone, in just the way you do.
   I give my tongue to speak your words,
   to spread your name and freedom-giving truth.

3. I give my mind in every way
   so that each thought I have will come from you.
   I give my spirit to you, Lord,
   and every day my prayer will spring anew.

4. I give my heart that you may love
   in me your Father and the human race.
   I give myself that you may grow
   in me and make my life a song of praise.

132 Susan Sayers

1. I have a friend who is deeper than the ocean,
   I have a friend who is wider than the sky,
   I have a friend who always understands me,
   whether I'm happy or ready to cry.

2. If I am lost he will search until he finds me,
   if I am scared he will help me to be brave.
   All I've to do is to turn to him and ask him.
   I know he'll honour the promise he gave.

3. 'Don't be afraid,' Jesus said, 'for I am with you.'
   'Don't be afraid,' Jesus said, 'for I am here.
   Now and for ever, anywhere you travel,
   I shall be with you, I'll be always near.'

133 Mike Burn

I love to be with you, Jesus,
list'ning to your voice,
and when I hear you speak my name
my heart and soul rejoice.
And if you said jump, I'd jump for you,
and if you said run, I'd run to your side,
and if you said leap, I'd take a leap of faith,
and if you said dance, I'd dance for sheer delight!
To be with you, to be with you,
to be with you, oh, it's the best thing;
to be with you, to be with you,
to be with you, it's the best thing in my life.

134 Rob Hayward

I'm accepted, I'm forgiven,
I am fathered by the true and living God.
I'm accepted, no condemnation,
I am loved by the true and living God.
There's no guilt or fear as I draw near
to the Saviour and creator of the world.
There is joy and peace as I release
my worship to you, O Lord.

135 Michael Forster

1. I'm black, I'm white, I'm short, I'm tall,
   I'm all the human race.
   I'm young, I'm old, I'm large, I'm small,
   and Jesus knows my face.

   The love of God is free to everyone,
   free to everyone,
   free to everyone.
   The love of God is free, oh yes!
   That's what the gospel says.

2. I'm rich, I'm poor, I'm pleased, I'm sad,
   I'm everyone you see.
   I'm quick, I'm slow, I'm good, I'm bad,
   I know that God loves me.

3. So tall and thin, and short and wide,
   and any shade of face,
   I'm one of those for whom Christ died,
   part of the human race.

136 Kevin Nichols

1. In bread we bring you, Lord,
   our bodies' labour.
   In wine we offer you
   our spirits' grief.
   We do not ask you, Lord,
   who is my neighbour,
   but stand united now,
   one in belief.
   O we have gladly heard
   your Word, your holy Word,
   and now in answer, Lord,
   our gifts we bring.
   Our selfish hearts make true,
   our failing faith renew,
   our lives belong to you,
   our Lord and King.

2. The bread we offer you
   is blessed and broken,
   and it becomes for us
   our spirit's food.
   Over the cup we bring
   your Word is spoken;
   make it your gift to us,
   your healing blood.
   Take all that daily toil
   plants in our heart's poor soil,
   take all we start and spoil,
   each hopeful dream,
   the chances we have missed,
   the graces we resist,
   Lord, in thy Eucharist,
   take and redeem.

137 Estelle White

1. In the love of God and neighbour
   we are gathered at his table:
   gifts of bread and wine will become a sign
   of the love our Father gave us,
   through the Son who came to save us,
   by the Spirit blest.

2. So we offer our tomorrows,
   all our present joys and sorrows,
   every heart and will, talent, gift and skill.
   For the riches we've been given
   to the Trinity of heaven
   we give thanks and praise.

138 Gerard Fitzpatrick

1. In the upper room, Jesus and his friends
   met to celebrate their final supper.
   Jesus took a bowl, knelt to wash their feet,
   told them:
   'You must do for others as I do for you.'

2. Peter was annoyed: 'This will never do!
   You, as Master, should not play the servant!'
   Jesus took a towel, knelt to dry their feet,
   told them:
   'You must do for others as I do for you.'

139 Francesca Leftley

1. In you, my God, may my soul find its peace;
   you are my refuge, my rock, and my strength,
   calming my fears with the touch of your love.
   Here in your presence my troubles will cease.

2. In you, my God, may my soul find its joy;
   you are the radiance, the song of my heart,
   drying my tears with the warmth of your love.
   Here in your presence my sorrow will cease.

3. In you, my God, may my soul find its rest;
   you are the meaning, the purpose of life,
   drawing me near to the fire of your love,
   safe in your presence my yearning will cease.

140 Judy Bailey

I reach up high, I touch the ground,
I stomp my feet and I turn around.
I've got to (woo woo) praise the Lord.
I jump and dance with all my might,
I might look funny but that's alright.
I've got to (woo woo) praise the Lord.

1. I'll do anything just for my God,
   'cause he's done everything for me.
   It doesn't matter who is looking on;
   Jesus is the person that I want to please.

2. May my whole life be a song of praise,
   to worship God in every way.
   In this song the actions praise his name,
   I want my actions every day to do the same.

141 Alan J. Price

Isn't it good to be together,
being with friends old and new?
Isn't it good? The Bible tells us
Jesus our Lord is here too!
Isn't it good to be together,
being with friends old and new?
Isn't it good? The Bible tells us
Jesus our Lord is here too!
He's here! By his Spirit he's with us.
He's here! His promise is true.
He's here! Though we can't see him,
he's here for me and you.
He's here! By his Spirit he's with us.
He's here! His promise is true.
He's here! Though we can't see him,
he's here for me and you.

142 Dan Schutte

1. I, the Lord of sea and sky,
   I have heard my people cry.
   All who dwell in dark and sin,
   my hand will save.
   I, who made the stars of night,
   I will make their darkness bright.
   Who will bear my light to them?
   Whom shall I send?

   Here I am, Lord. Is it I, Lord?
   I have heard you calling in the night.
   I will go, Lord, if you lead me.
   I will hold your people in my heart.

Continued overleaf

2. I, the Lord of snow and rain,
   I have borne my people's pain.
   I have wept for love of them.
   They turn away.
   I will break their hearts of stone,
   give them hearts for love alone.
   I will speak my word to them.
   Whom shall I send?

   Here I am, Lord. Is it I, Lord?
   I have heard you calling in the night.
   I will go, Lord, if you lead me.
   I will hold your people in my heart.

3. I, the Lord of wind and flame,
   I will tend the poor and lame.
   I will set a feast for them.
   My hand will save.
   Finest bread I will provide,
   till their hearts are satisfied.
   I will give my life to them.
   Whom shall I send?

143 Spiritual

1. I've got peace like a river,
   I've got peace like a river,
   I've got peace like a river in my soul.

2. I've got joy like a fountain . . .

3. I've got love like an ocean . . .

144 Graham Jeffery

I want to build my life on the Lord, my God,
build my life on the Lord,
I want to build my life, I want to build my life,
I want to build my life on the Lord.

1. I'll love him,
   love him,
   love him,
   love him.

2. I'll praise him,
   praise him,
   praise him,
   praise him.

3. I'll thank him,
   thank him,
   thank him,
   thank him.

145 Michael Forster

Lines in ordinary type are sung by the leader; those in
bold type by everybody.

1. I was so glad,
   I was so glad,
   when they said to me,
   when they said to me,
   'Let us go up,
   let us go up,
   to the house of God,
   to the house of God.'

Continued overleaf

I was so glad when they said to me,
'Let us go up to the house of God.'
Now we shall stand,
now we shall stand in Jerusalem!

2. Solidly built,
   solidly built,
   is Jerusalem,
   is Jerusalem.
   There we shall go,
   There we shall go,
   people of the Lord,
   people of the Lord.

3. Here by his law,
   here by his law,
   God is glorified,
   God is glorified.
   Judgement is his,
   Judgement is his,
   on King David's throne,
   on King David's throne.

146 John Glynn

1. I watch the sunrise lighting the sky,
   casting its shadows near.
   And on this morning, bright though it be,
   I feel those shadows near me.

   But you are always close to me,
   following all my ways.
   May I be always close to you,
   following all your ways, Lord.

2. I watch the sunlight shine through the clouds,
   warming the earth below.
   And at midday, life seems to say:
   'I feel your brightness near me.'

   For you are always . . .

3. I watch the sunset fading away,
   lighting the clouds with sleep.
   And as the evening closes its eyes,
   I feel your presence near me.

   For you are always . . .

4. I watch the moonlight guarding the night,
   waiting till morning comes.
   The air is silent, earth is at rest
   – only your peace is near me.

   Yes, you are always . . .

147 Gerard Markland

I will be with you wherever you go.
Go now throughout the world!
I will be with you in all that you say.
Go now and spread my word!

1. Come, walk with me on stormy waters.
   Why fear? Reach out, and I'll be there.

2. And you, my friend, will you now leave me,
   or do you know me as your Lord?

Continued overleaf

3. Your life will be transformed with power
   by living truly in my name.

   I will be with you wherever you go.
   Go now throughout the world!
   I will be with you in all that you say.
   Go now and spread my word!

4. And if you say, 'Yes, Lord, I love you',
   then feed my lambs and feed my sheep.

148 Susan Sayers

I will bless the Lord at all times.
I will bless the Lord at all times.

1. Everywhere I am, everywhere I go,
   I will praise the living God.
   In everyone I meet,
   in everything I see
   I will sing your praise, O Lord.

2. When I was in pain, when I lived in fear,
   I was calling out to him.
   He rescued me from death, he wiped my tears away,
   I will sing your praise, O Lord.

3. Trust him with your life, trust him with today,
   come and praise the Lord with me;
   O come and know his love, O taste and understand,
   let us sing your praise, O Lord.

149 Ian Smale

I will click my fingers, clap my hands,
stamp my feet and shout hallelujah!
Then I'll whistle as loud as I can.
(Whistle)
I'm happy I'm a child of the Lord.

© 1989 Glorie Music/Kingsway's Thankyou Music

150 Leona von Brethorst

I will enter his gates with thanksgiving in my heart,
I will enter his courts with praise.
I will say this is the day that the Lord has made.
I will rejoice for he has made me glad.
He has made me glad.
He has made me glad.
I will rejoice for he has made me glad.
He has made me glad.
He has made me glad.
I will rejoice for he has made me glad.

© 1976 Maranatha! Music/CopyCare

151 Max Dyer

1. I will sing, I will sing a song unto the Lord.
   I will sing, I will sing a song unto the Lord.
   I will sing, I will sing a song unto the Lord.
   Alleluia, glory to the Lord.

2. We will come, we will come as one before the Lord.
   We will come, we will come as one before the Lord.
   We will come, we will come as one before the Lord.
   Alleluia, glory to the Lord.

Continued overleaf

3. If the Son, if the Son shall make you free,
   if the Son, if the Son shall make you free,
   if the Son, if the Son shall make you free,
   you shall be free indeed.

4. They that sow in tears shall reap in joy.
   They that sow in tears shall reap in joy.
   They that sow in tears shall reap in joy.
   Alleluia, glory to the Lord.

5. Every knee shall bow and every tongue confess,
   every knee shall bow and every tongue confess,
   every knee shall bow and every tongue confess
   that Jesus Christ is Lord.

6. In his name, in his name we have the victory.
   In his name, in his name we have the victory.
   In his name, in his name we have the victory.
   Alleluia, glory to the Lord.

152 Ian Smale

I will wave my hands in praise and adoration,
I will wave my hands in praise and adoration,
I will wave my hands in praise and adoration,
praise and adoration to the living God.

For he's given me hands that just love clapping:
one, two, one, two, three;
and he's given me a voice that just loves shouting,
'Hallelujah!'

He's given me feet that just love dancing:
one, two, one, two, three;
and he's put me in a being
that has no trouble seeing
that whatever I am feeling
he is worthy to be praised.

153 Delores Dufner

Jesus, ever-flowing fountain,
Give us water from your well.
In the gracious gift you offer
There is joy no tongue can tell.

1. Come to me, all pilgrims thirsty,
   drink the water I will give.
   If you knew what gift I offer,
   you would come to me and live.

2. Come to me, all trav'lers weary,
   come that I may give you rest.
   Drink the cup of life I offer;
   at this table be my guest.

3. Come to me, believers burdened,
   find refreshment in this place.
   If you knew the gift I offer,
   you would turn and seek my face.

154 Michael Forster

Jesus had all kinds of friends,
so the gospel stories say.
Jesus had all kinds of friends,
and there's room for us today.

1. Some were happy, some were sad,
   some were good and some were bad,
   some were short and some were tall,
   Jesus said he loved them all.

2. Some were humble, some were proud,
   some were quiet, some were loud,
   some were fit and some were lame,
   Jesus loved them all the same.

3. Some were healthy, some were sick,
   some were slow and some were quick,
   some were clever, some were not,
   Jesus said he loved the lot!

155 Gill Hutchinson

Jesus is greater than the greatest heroes,
Jesus is closer than the closest friends.
He came from heaven and he died to save us,
to show us love that never ends.
Jesus is greater than the greatest heroes,
Jesus is closer than the closest friends.
He came from heaven and he died to save us,
to show us love that never ends.

Son of God, and Lord of glory,
he's the light, follow in his way.
He's the truth that we can believe in,
and he's the life, he's living today.
Son of God, and Lord of glory,
he's the light, follow in his way.
He's the truth that we can believe in,
and he's the life, he's living today.

156 H. W. Rattle

Jesus' love is very wonderful,
Jesus' love is very wonderful,
Jesus' love is very wonderful,
oh wonderful love!
So high you can't get over it,
so low you can't get under it,
so wide you can't get round it,
oh wonderful love!

157 Graham Kendrick

1. Jesus put this song into our hearts,
   Jesus put this song into our hearts;
   it's a song of joy no one can take away.
   Jesus put this song into our hearts.

2. Jesus taught us how to live in harmony,
   Jesus taught us how to live in harmony;
   different faces, different races, he made us one.
   Jesus taught us how to live in harmony.

Continued overleaf

3. Jesus turned our sorrow into dancing,
   Jesus turned our sorrow into dancing;
   changed our tears of sadness into rivers of joy.
   Jesus turned our sorrow into a dance.

158 Luke 23:42

Jesus, remember me
when you come into your kingdom.
Jesus, remember me
when you come into your kingdom.

159 Damian Lundy

1. Jesus rose on Easter Day:
   Alleluia, now we pray!
   Resurrexit, let us say,
   for he is Lord and mighty God for ever.

2. He has conquered death and sin.
   All God's people now begin
   singing praises unto him,
   for he is Lord and mighty God for ever.

3. 'Alleluia' is our cry,
   for he lives, no more to die.
   Glory be to God on high,
   for he is Lord and mighty God for ever.

4. Alleluia! May we know
   all the joy which long ago
   set the Easter sky aglow,
   for he is Lord and mighty God for ever.

5. Alleluia! Let us be
   filled with love, our hearts set free
   as we praise his victory,
   for he is Lord and mighty God for ever.

160 Michael Forster

1. Jesus went away to the desert, praying,
   listened for his Father's voice.
   Then he heard the voice of the tempter saying,
   'Why not make the easy choice?'

   Ain't list'nin' to no temptation,
   ain't fallin' for no persuasion,
   ain't gonna turn away from salvation,
   I'm a-waitin' on the word of the Lord.

2. 'There's an easy way if you'd only choose it,
   you can turn the stones to bread!
   What's the good of pow'r if you don't abuse it?
   Gotta keep yourself well fed!'

3. 'What about a stunt to attract attention,
   showing off your special pow'r?
   You'd get more applause than I'd care to mention
   jumping from the Temple tow'r!'

4. 'Everything you want will be right there for you,
   listen to the words I say!
   Nobody who matters will dare ignore you;
   my way is the easy way.'

161 Greg Leavers

Jesus will never, ever,
no not ever, never, ever change.
He will always, always,
that's for all days,
always be the same;
so as Son of God
and King of kings
he will for ever reign.
Yesterday, today, for ever,
Jesus is the same.
Yesterday, today, for ever,
Jesus is the same.

162 David Hind

Jesus, you love me more than I can know.
Jesus, you love me more than words can say.
I'm special, I'm planned;
I'm born with a future,
I'm in your hands.
I'm forgiven,
I've been changed;
loved by my Father
who knows me by name.
I'm loved by my Father
who knows me by name.

163 Michael Forster

1. Join the song of praise and protest,
   all the nations of the earth:
   God, who loves the poor and humble,
   sings of dignity and worth.
   Those the world has long rejected
   take at last their rightful place,
   sharing in the song of Mary,
   filled with unexpected grace.

   Magnificat, magnificat,
   praise the Lord, my soul;
   magnificat, magnificat,
   praise the Lord, my soul.

2. God has rocked the earth's foundations,
   turned its values upside-down:
   strength is overcome by weakness
   and the humble wear the crown.
   Now the pow'r of God in action
   undermines the nations' pride,
   lifts the poor and feeds the hungry,
   pushing rich and proud aside.

3. Join the song of praise and protest
   as the voiceless find a voice,
   as the pow'rless rise triumphant
   and the broken hearts rejoice.
   Now the God of all creation
   rights the long-accepted wrongs;
   let the voices of the nations
   swell the liberation song.

164 Marie Lydia Pereira

1. Joseph was an honest man,
   he was an honest man.
   He pleased the Lord in all his ways
   because he was an honest man;
   and God said: 'I am choosing you,
   because you are an honest man,
   to care for the one who'll bear my son,
   because you are an honest man.'

2. Joseph was a faithful man,
   he was a faithful man.
   He kept the trust the Lord had given
   because he was a faithful man.
   He cared for Mary and her son,
   because he was a faithful man,
   through days of pain and days of fun,
   because he was a faithful man.

3. Joseph was a working man,
   he was a working man.
   He laboured as a carpenter
   because he was a working man.
   And daily at his work he'd be,
   because he was a working man,
   no idler or a shirker he,
   because he was a working man.

4. Joseph was a praying man,
   he was a praying man.
   He walked with God each single day
   because he was a praying man.
   In joy or pain he'd turn to him,
   because he was a praying man,
   if fear did rage or hope grow dim,
   because he was a praying man.

5. Joseph was an honest man,
   he was an honest man.
   His blameless life won its reward
   because he was an honest man.
   The Lord was pleased and called him home,
   because he was an honest man,
   with him to rest, no more to roam,
   because he was an honest man.

6. Joseph is a helping man,
   he is a helping man.
   He rescues those who turn to him
   because he is a helping man.
   So go to Joseph in your need,
   because he is a helping man,
   you'll see him work with speed and power,
   because he is a helping man.

165 Fred Dunn

Jubilate, everybody,
serve the Lord in all your ways
and come before his presence singing,
enter now his courts with praise.
For the Lord our God is gracious,
and his mercy everlasting.
Jubilate, jubilate,
jubilate Deo!

166 Susan Sayers

1. Just imagine having a world
   where people care,
   glad to help
   and loving in word and deed.

   Well, it can be true
   if we really want it to,
   and the love of Jesus living in us
   is all we need.

2. Just imagine having a world
   where people care,
   glad to give
   without any hate or greed.

167 Sophie Conty and Naomi Batya

King of kings and Lord of lords.
Glory, hallelujah!
King of kings and Lord of lords.
Glory, hallelujah!
Jesus, Prince of Peace.
Glory, hallelujah!
Jesus, Prince of Peace.
Glory, hallelujah!

168 Spiritual

1. Kum ba yah, my Lord, kum ba yah,
   kum ba yah, my Lord, kum ba yah,
   kum ba yah, my Lord, kum ba yah,
   O Lord, kum ba yah.

2. Someone's crying, Lord, kum ba yah . . .

3. Someone's singing, Lord, kum ba yah . . .

4. Someone's praying, Lord, kum ba yah . . .

169 Taizé Community

Latin text

Laudate Dominum,
laudate Dominum,
omnes gentes, alleluia!
Laudate Dominum,
laudate Dominum,
omnes gentes, alleluia!

English text

Sing, praise and bless the Lord.
Sing, praise and bless the Lord!
Peoples! Nations! Alleluia!
Sing, praise and bless the Lord.
Sing, praise and bless the Lord!
Peoples! Nations! Alleluia!

Damian Lundy, after St Francis of Assisi

Laudato sii, O mi Signore.
Laudato sii, O mi Signore.
Laudato sii, O mi Signore.
Laudato sii, O mi Signore.

1. Yes, be praised in all your creatures,
   sun our brother, moon our sister,
   in the stars and in the breezes,
   air and fire and flowing water.

2. Thank you for the earth, our mother,
   she who feeds us and sustains us;
   for her fruits, her grass, her flowers,
   for the mountains and the oceans.

3. Praise for those who spread forgiveness,
   those who share your peace with others,
   bearing trials and sickness bravely.
   Even sister death won't harm them.

4. Life is but a song of worship,
   and the reason for our singing
   is to praise you for the music,
   join the dance of all creation!

5. Praise be to you, our God and Father,
   praise and thanks to you, Lord Jesus,
   praise to you, most Holy Spirit,
   life and joy of all creation!

   After the last refrain add:
   Laudato sii!

The Italian phrase 'Laudato sii, O mi Signore' translates as 'Praise be to you, O my Lord'.

171 Carey Landry

Lay your hands gently upon us,
let their touch render your peace,
let them bring your forgiveness and healing,
lay your hands, gently lay your hands.

1. You were sent to free the broken-hearted.
   You were sent to give sight to the blind.
   You desire to heal all our illness.
   Lay your hands, gently lay your hands.

2. Lord, we come to you through one another.
   Lord, we come to you in all our need.
   Lord, we come to you seeking wholeness.
   Lay your hands, gently lay your hands.

172 Michael Forster

1. Let love be real, in giving and receiving,
   without the need to manage and to own;
   a haven, free from posing and pretending,
   where every weakness may be safely known.
   Give me your hand, along the desert pathway,
   give me your love wherever we may go.
   As God loves us, so let us love each other:
   with no demands, just open hands
   and space to grow.

Continued overleaf

2. Let love be real, not grasping or confining,
   that strange embrace that holds yet sets us free;
   that helps us face the risk of truly living,
   and makes us brave to be what we might be.
   Give me your strength when all my words are
        weakness;
   give me your love in spite of all you know.
   As God loves us, so let us love each other:
   with no demands, just open hands
   and space to grow.

3. Let love be real, with no manipulation,
   no secret wish to harness or control.
   Let us accept each other's incompleteness,
   and share the joy of learning to be whole.
   Give me your hope through dreams and
        disappointments,
   give me your trust when all my failings show.
   As God loves us, so let us love each other:
   with no demands, just open hands
   and space to grow.

© 1995 Kevin Mayhew Ltd.

173 Bryan Spinks

Let our praise to you be as incense,
let us bless your holy name;
let our praise to you be as incense,
as your glory we proclaim.
May our voices join with the angels
as we praise your holy name:
holy, holy, holy is the Lord almighty,
who was, and is, and is to come.

© 1996 Kevin Mayhew Ltd.

174 Susan Sayers

1. Let the mountains dance and sing!
   Let the trees all sway and swing!
   All creation praise its King!
   Alleluia!

2. Let the water sing its song!
   And the pow'rful wind so strong
   whistle as it blows along!
   Alleluia!

3. Let the blossom all break out
   in a huge unspoken shout,
   just to show that God's about!
   Alleluia!

175 Fred Kaan

1. Let us talents and tongues employ,
   reaching out with a shout of joy:
   bread is broken, the wine is poured,
   Christ is spoken and seen and heard.

   Jesus lives again,
   earth can breathe again,
   pass the word around:
   loaves abound!

2. Christ is able to make us one,
   at the table he sets the tone,
   teaching people to live to bless,
   love in word and in deed express.

Continued overleaf

3. Jesus calls us in, sends us out
   bearing fruit in a world of doubt,
   gives us love to tell, bread to share:
   God-Immanuel everywhere!

   Jesus lives again,
   earth can breathe again,
   pass the word around:
   loaves abound!

176 Michael Forster

1. Life for the poor was hard and tough,
   Jesus said, 'That's not good enough;
   life should be great and here's the sign:
   I'll turn the water into wine.'

   Jesus turned the water into wine, (3)
   and the people saw that life was good.

2. Life is a thing to be enjoyed,
   not to be wasted or destroyed.
   Laughter is part of God's design;
   let's turn the water into wine!

3. Go to the lonely and the sad,
   give them the news to make them glad,
   helping the light of hope to shine,
   turning the water into wine!

177 W. L. Wallace

1. Life is for living now;
   not moaning or groaning,
   avoiding, disowning:
   life is for living now!

2. Life is for living now;
   not killing or caging,
   destroying or grasping:
   life is for living now!

3. Life is for living now;
   for feeling and thinking,
   for growing and finding:
   life is for living now!

4. Life is for living now;
   for praying and serving,
   for living and loving:
   life is for living now!

5. Life is for living now;
   for healing and freeing,
   rejoicing and dancing:
   life is for living now!

178 Carey Landry

Like a sunflower that follows
every movement of the sun,
so I turn toward you
to follow you, my God.

1. In simplicity, charity, I follow.
   In simplicity, charity, I follow.

2. In simplicity, honesty, I follow.
   In simplicity, honesty, I follow.

3. In simplicity, fidelity, I follow.
   In simplicity, fidelity, I follow.

179 Aniceto Nazareth

Listen, let your heart keep seeking;
listen to his constant speaking;
listen to the Spirit calling you.
Listen to his inspiration;
listen to his invitation;
listen to the Spirit calling you.

1. He's in the sound of the thunder,
   in the whisper of the breeze.
   He's in the might of the whirlwind,
   in the roaring of the seas.

2. He's in the laughter of children,
   in the patter of the rain.
   Hear him in the cries of the suff'ring,
   in their sorrow and their pain.

3. He's in the noise of the city,
   in the singing of the birds.
   And in the night-time, the stillness
   helps you listen to his word.

180 Patrick Appleford

1. Lord Jesus Christ,
   you have come to us,
   you are one with us,
   Mary's Son.
   Cleansing our souls from all their sin,
   pouring your love and goodness in,
   Jesus, our love for you we sing,
   living Lord.

2. Lord Jesus Christ,
   now and every day
   teach us how to pray,
   Son of God.
   You have commanded us to do
   this in remembrance, Lord, of you,
   into our lives your pow'r breaks through,
   living Lord.

3. Lord Jesus Christ,
   you have come to us,
   born as one of us,
   Mary's Son.
   Led out to die on Calvary,
   risen from death to set us free,
   living Lord Jesus, help us see
   you are Lord.

Continued overleaf

4. Lord Jesus Christ,
   I would come to you,
   live my life for you,
   Son of God.
   All your commands I know are true,
   your many gifts will make me new,
   into my life your pow'r breaks through,
   living Lord.

181 Jan Struther

1. Lord of all hopefulness,
   Lord of all joy,
   whose trust, ever childlike,
   no cares could destroy,
   be there at our waking
   and give us, we pray,
   your bliss in our hearts, Lord,
   at the break of the day.

2. Lord of all eagerness,
   Lord of all faith,
   whose strong hands were skilled
   at the plane and the lathe,
   be there at our labours
   and give us, we pray,
   your strength in our hearts, Lord,
   at the noon of the day.

3. Lord of all kindliness,
   Lord of all grace,
   your hands swift to welcome,
   your arms to embrace,
   be there at our homing
   and give us we pray,
   your love in our hearts, Lord,
   at the eve of the day.

4. Lord of all gentleness,
   Lord of all calm,
   whose voice is contentment,
   whose presence is balm,
   be there at our sleeping
   and give us, we pray,
   your peace in our hearts, Lord,
   at the end of the day.

182 Hubert J. Richards

Leader: Lord of creation, may your will be done.

All: Lord of creation, may your will be done.

183 Patrick Appleford

1. Lord of life,
   you give us all our days:
   let your life
   fill ours with hope and praise.
   May our learning,
   seeking, yearning,
   lead us on to share
   your risen life.

Continued overleaf

2. 'Come to me,
   and I will give you rest.'
   Help us see
   your way is richly blest;
   guide our questing,
   working, resting,
   till we hear you calling,
   'Follow me'.

3. Lord, we come,
   encouraged by your grace,
   Lord, we come,
   and things fall into place,
   pilgrims ever,
   we endeavour,
   Lord, to follow as you
   bring us home.

4. Lord, may we
   bring all our strength and skill;
   help us be
   prepared to do your will.
   Turn our living
   into giving
   love and service as you
   set us free.

5. Glory be
   to God for all his love;
   here may we
   with saints below, above,
   go rejoicing,
   ever voicing
   praise for such a welcome,
   'Come to me'.

184 Ian D. Craig

1. Lord of the future,
   Lord of the past,
   Lord of our lives, we adore you.
   Lord of forever,
   Lord of our hearts,
   we give all praise to you.

2. Lord of tomorrow,
   Lord of today,
   Lord over all, you are worthy.
   Lord of creation,
   Lord of all truth,
   we give all praise to you.

185 Graham Kendrick

1. Lord, the light of your love is shining,
   in the midst of the darkness, shining,
   Jesus, Light of the World, shine upon us,
   set us free by the truth you now bring us,
   shine on me, shine on me.

   Shine, Jesus, shine,
   fill this land with the Father's glory;
   blaze, Spirit, blaze,
   set our hearts on fire.
   Flow, river, flow,
   flood the nations with grace and mercy;
   send forth your word, Lord,
   and let there be light!

Continued overleaf

2. Lord, I come to your awesome presence,
   from the shadows into your radiance;
   by the blood I may enter your brightness,
   search me, try me, consume all my darkness.
   Shine on me, shine on me.

   Shine, Jesus, shine,
   fill this land with the Father's glory;
   blaze, Spirit, blaze,
   set our hearts on fire.
   Flow, river, flow,
   flood the nations with grace and mercy;
   send forth your word, Lord,
   and let there be light!

3. As we gaze on your kingly brightness,
   so our faces display your likeness,
   ever changing from glory to glory,
   mirrored here, may our lives tell your story.
   Shine on me, shine on me.

186 Ian Smale

Lord, we've come to worship you,
Lord, we've come to praise;
Lord, we've come to worship you
in oh so many ways.
Some of us shout and some of us sing,
and some of us whisper the praise we bring,
but, Lord, we all are gathering
to give you our praise.

187 Alan J. Price

Lord, you've promised, through your Son,
you'll forgive the wrongs we've done;
we confess them, every one,
please, dear Lord, forgive us.

1. Things we've done and things we've said,
   we regret the hurt they spread.
   Lord, we're sorry.
   Lord, we're sorry.

2. Sinful and unkind thoughts too,
   all of these are known to you.
   Lord, we're sorry.
   Lord, we're sorry.

3. And the things we've left undone,
   words and deeds we should have done.
   Lord, we're sorry.
   Lord, we're sorry.

   Last refrain:
   Lord, you've promised, through your Son,
   you'll forgive the wrong we've done;
   we receive your pardon,
   Lord, as you forgive us.

188 Michael Forster

1. Love is the only law, for God and humankind:
   love your God with all your heart, your strength
       and soul and mind.
   Love your neighbour as yourself, of every creed
       and race,
   turn the water of endless laws into the wine of grace.

Continued overleaf

Love is God's only law, love is God's only law,
Love is God's wisdom, love is God's strength,
love of such height, such depth, such length,
love is God's only law.

2. Give to the poor a voice and help the blind to see,
feed the hungry, heal the sick and set the captive free.
All that God requires of you will then fall into place,
turn the water of endless laws into the wine of grace.

3. Let love like fountains flow and justice like a stream,
faith become reality and hope your constant theme.
Then shall freedom, joy and peace, with
    righteousness embrace,
turn the water of endless laws into the wine of grace.

189 Luke Connaughton

1. Love is his word, love is his way,
feasting with all, fasting alone,
living and dying, rising again,
love, only love, is his way.

*Richer than gold is the love of my Lord:
better than splendour and wealth.*

2. Love is his way, love is his mark,
sharing his last Passover feast,
Christ at the table, host to the twelve,
love, only love, is his mark.

3. Love is his mark, love is his sign,
bread for our strength, wine for our joy,
'This is my body, this is my blood.'
Love, only love, is his sign.

4. Love is his sign, love is his news,
   'Do this,' he said, 'lest you forget
   all my deep sorrow, all my dear blood.'
   Love, only love, is his news.

5. Love is his news, love is his name,
   we are his own, chosen and called,
   family, brethren, cousins and kin.
   Love, only love, is his law.

6. Love is his name, love is his law,
   hear his command, all who are his,
   'Love one another, I have loved you.'
   Love, only love, is his law.

7. Love is his law, love is his word:
   love of the Lord, Father and Word,
   love of the Spirit, God ever one,
   love, only love, is his word.

190 W. L. Wallace

Love is (clap) like a circle (clap),
we can join it (clap) anywhere (clap).
Let's take our courage in our hands
and lay aside despair.

1. Sometimes it's our neighbour (clap),
   sometimes those at play (clap),
   sometimes those we work with (clap),
   or with whom we pray.

Continued overleaf

2. Sometimes it's a granny,
   mother or a dad,
   sometimes it's a baby,
   smiling or so sad.

   Love is (clap) like a circle (clap),
   we can join it (clap) anywhere (clap).
   Let's take our courage in our hands
   and lay aside despair.

3. Love can come from adults
   and from girls and boys;
   love can come in silence
   or within the noise.

4. Some find love through list'ning,
   some through ardent prayer,
   others in the scriptures,
   some through tender care.

5. Love can make us happy,
   love can bring us tears,
   love can make us peaceful,
   casting out our fears.

   Last refrain:

   But in all our loving,
   from beginning to the end,
   the love we share all comes from God
   who greets us in each friend.

191   Sister Patrick Ignatius

Love is patient,
Love is always kind,
love can take the roughest path
and never seem to mind.
Love is never boastful
or jealous of the rest,
love is strong and faces every test.

1. If I speak with eloquence
   and make the angels stare,
   I'm a tinkling cymbal,
   if love is never there.
   If I am a prophet
   and know all things to come,
   if I have not love,
   I might as well be dumb!

2. If my faith is strong, then I
   might make the mountains move,
   feed the hungry people,
   but what does that all prove?
   I can give up all things –
   possessions come and go –
   but unless there's love
   it doesn't count, I know.

3. Love goes on for evermore
   but prophesies will pass;
   tongues will cease their wagging,
   and knowledge will not last;
   for we know so little,
   and the future's very dim,
   but with faith and hope,
   our love leads us on to him.

192 Scripture

Magnificat, magnificat
anima mea Dominum.
Magnificat, magnificat
anima mea Dominum.

Translation: My soul praises and magnifies the Lord.

193 Sebastian Temple

1. Make me a channel of your peace.
   Where there is hatred, let me bring your love.
   Where there is injury, your pardon, Lord,
   and where there's doubt, true faith in you.

2. Make me a channel of your peace.
   Where there's despair in life, let me bring hope.
   Where there is darkness, only light,
   and where there's sadness, ever joy.

3. O Master, grant that I may never seek
   so much to be consoled as to console,
   to be understood, as to understand,
   to be loved, as to love with all my soul.

4. Make me a channel of your peace.
   It is in pardoning that we are pardoned,
   in giving of ourselves that we receive,
   and in dying that we're born to eternal life.

194 Eleanor Farjeon

1. Morning has broken
   like the first morning,
   blackbird has spoken
   like the first bird.
   Praise for the singing!
   Praise for the morning!
   Praise for them, springing
   fresh from the Word!

2. Sweet the rain's new fall,
   sunlit from heaven,
   like the first dew-fall
   on the first grass.
   Praise for the sweetness
   of the wet garden,
   sprung in completeness
   where his feet pass.

3. Mine is the sunlight!
   Mine is the morning,
   born of the one light
   Eden saw play.
   Praise with elation,
   praise every morning,
   God's re-creation
   of the new day!

1. 'Moses, I know you're the man,'
   the Lord said.
   'You're going to work out my plan,'
   the Lord said.
   'Lead all the Israelites out of slavery,
   and I shall make them a wandering race
   called the people of God.'

   So every day we're on our way,
   for we're a travelling, wandering race
   called the people of God.

2. 'Don't get too set in your ways,'
   the Lord said.
   'Each step is only a phase,'
   the Lord said.
   'I'll go before you and I shall be a sign
   to guide my travelling, wandering race.
   You're the people of God.'

3. 'No matter what you may do,'
   the Lord said,
   'I shall be faithful and true,'
   the Lord said.
   'My love will strengthen you as you go along,
   for you're my travelling, wandering race.
   You're the people of God.'

4. 'Look at the birds of the air,'
   the Lord said.
   'They fly unhampered by care,'
   the Lord said.
   'You will move easier if you're travelling light,
   for you're a travelling, vagabond race.
   You're the people of God.'

5. 'Foxes have places to go,'
   the Lord said,
   'but I've no home here below,'
   the Lord said.
   'So if you want to be with me all your days,
   keep up the moving and travelling on.
   You're the people of God.'

196 v 1 unknown, vv 2-5 Sandra Joan Billington

1. My God loves me,
   his love will never end.
   He rests within my heart,
   for my God loves me.

2. His gentle hand
   he stretches over me.
   Though storm-clouds threaten the day,
   he will set me free.

3. He comes to me
   in sharing bread and wine.
   He brings me life that will reach
   past the end of time.

4. My God loves me,
   his faithful love endures,
   and I will live like a child
   held in love secure.

5. The joys of love
   as off'rings now we bring.
   The pains of love will be lost
   in the praise we sing.

197 Ian Smale

1. My mouth was made for worship,
   my hands were made to raise,
   my feet were made for dancing,
   my life is one of praise to Jesus.
   And all God's people said: Amen,
   hallelujah, amen, praise and glory,
   amen, amen, amen, amen.
   wo, wo, wo, wo.

2. My heart was made for loving,
   my mind to know God's ways,
   my body was made a temple,
   my life is one of praise to Jesus.
   And all God's people said: Amen,
   hallelujah, amen, praise and glory,
   amen, amen, amen, amen.
   wo, wo, wo, wo, wo.

198 Verse 1 Scripture/Verses 2-4 Damian Lundy

1. My soul doth magnify the Lord,
   and my spirit hath rejoiced in God my Saviour,
   for he that is mighty hath done great things,
   and holy is his name.

   My soul doth magnify the Lord,
   my soul doth magnify the Lord,
   and my spirit hath rejoiced in God my Saviour,
   for he that is mighty hath done great things,
   and holy is his name.

2. From age to age he shows his love,
   and his mercy is for ever to his servants,
   for he stretches out his arm, casts down the mighty,
   and raises up the meek.

3. He fills the hungry with good food.
   When the rich demand their share, their hands
      are empty.
   He has kept all his promises to Israel:
   his mercy is made known.

4. To God the Father we sing praise,
   and to Jesus, whom he sent to be our Saviour!
   To the Spirit of God be all glory,
   For holy is his name!

199 Anne Carter

1. My soul proclaims you, mighty God.
   My spirit sings your praise.
   You look on me, you lift me up,
   and gladness fills my days.

2. All nations now will share my joy;
   your gifts you have outpoured.
   Your little one you have made great;
   I magnify my God.

3. For those who love your holy name,
   your mercy will not die.
   Your strong right arm puts down the proud
   and lifts the lowly high.

Continued overleaf

4. You fill the hungry with good things,
   the rich you send away.
   The promise made to Abraham
   is filled to endless day.

5. Magnificat, magnificat,
   magnificat, praise God!
   Praise God, praise God, praise God, praise God,
   magnificat, praise God!

200 John Hardwick

1. Nobody's a nobody,
   believe me 'cause it's true.
   Nobody's a nobody,
   especially not you.
   Nobody's a nobody,
   and God wants us to see
   that everybody's somebody,
   and that means even me.

2. I'm no cartoon, I'm human,
   I have feelings, treat me right.
   I'm not a super hero
   with super strength and might.
   I'm not a mega pop star
   or super athlete,
   but did you know I'm special,
   in fact I'm quite unique!

3. Nobody's a nobody,
   believe me 'cause it's true.
   Nobody's a nobody,
   especially not you.
   Nobody's a nobody,
   and God wants us to see
   that everybody's somebody,
   and that means even me.

201 Graham Kendrick

1. O come and join the dance
   that all began so long ago,
   when Christ the Lord was born in Bethlehem.
   Through all the years of darkness
   still the dance goes on and on,
   oh, take my hand and come and join the song.

   Rejoice! (Rejoice!)
   Rejoice! (Rejoice!)
   O lift your voice and sing
   and open up your heart to welcome him.
   Rejoice! (Rejoice!)
   Rejoice! (Rejoice!)
   and welcome now your King,
   for Christ the Lord was born in Bethlehem.

2. Come, shed your heavy load
   and dance your worries away,
   for Christ the Lord was born in Bethlehem.
   He came to break the pow'r of sin
   and turn your night to day,
   oh, take my hand and come and join the song.

Continued overleaf

3. Let laughter ring and angels sing
and joy be all around,
for Christ the Lord was born in Bethlehem.
And if you seek with all your heart
he surely can be found,
oh, take my hand and come and join the song.

Rejoice! (Rejoice!)
Rejoice! (Rejoice!)
O lift your voice and sing
and open up your heart to him.
Rejoice! (Rejoice!)
Rejoice! (Rejoice!)
and welcome now your King,
for Christ the Lord was born in Bethlehem.

202 Kevin Mayhew

O, come to the water,
all you who are thirsty,
and drink, drink deeply.
Though you don't have a penny
and your clothes are in rags,
you'll be welcome to drink
all you can.

1. Come, take your choice of wine and milk:
everything here is free!
Why spend your money on worthless food?
Everything here is free!

2. Now, listen well and you will find
food that will feed your soul.
Just come to me to receive your share,
food that will feed your soul.

3. I promise you good things to come;
   you are my chosen ones.
   I name you witnesses to my world;
   you are my chosen ones.

203 Joanne Pond

O give thanks to the Lord,
all you his people,
O give thanks to the Lord,
for he is good.
Let us praise, let us thank,
let us celebrate and dance,
O give thanks to the Lord,
for he is good.

204 Francesca Leftley

1. Oh Mary, gentle one,
   teach us to love your Son.
   Oh Mary, humble one,
   help us to serve him.

   Teach us to answer him,
   as once you answered him:
   'Let it be done to me
   according to your word.'

2. Oh Mary, peaceful one,
   help us to know your Son.
   Oh Mary, hopeful one,
   teach us to trust him.

Continued overleaf

3. Oh Mary, grateful one,
   teach us to thank your Son.
   Oh Mary, joyful one,
   help us to praise him.

   Teach us to answer him,
   as once you answered him:
   'Let it be done to me
   according to your word.'

205 Unknown

Oh! Oh! Oh! how good is the Lord,
Oh! Oh! Oh! how good is the Lord,
Oh! Oh! Oh! how good is the Lord,
I never will forget what he has done for me.

1. He gives me salvation, how good is the Lord,
   he gives me salvation, how good is the Lord,
   he gives me salvation, how good is the Lord,
   I never will forget what he has done for me.

2. He gives me his blessings . . .

3. He gives me his Spirit . . .

4. He gives me his healing . . .

5. He gives me his glory . . .

206 Estelle White

1. O lady, full of God's own grace,
   whose caring hands the child embraced,
   who listened to the Spirit's word,
   believed and trusted in the Lord.

O virgin fair, star of the sea,
my dearest mother, pray for me.
O virgin fair, star of the sea,
my dearest mother, pray for me.

2. O lady, who felt daily joy
   in caring for the holy boy,
   whose home was plain and shorn of wealth,
   yet was enriched by God's own breath.

3. O lady, who bore living's pain
   but still believed that love would reign,
   who on a hill watched Jesus die,
   as on the cross they raised him high.

4. O lady, who, on Easter day,
   had all your sorrow wiped away
   as God the Father's will was done
   when from death's hold he freed your Son.

207 Virginia Vissing

O living water, refresh my soul.
O living water, refresh my soul.
Spirit of joy, Lord of creation.
Spirit of hope, Spirit of peace.

1. Spirit of God. Spirit of God.

2. O set us free. O set us free.

3. Come, pray in us. Come, pray in us.

208 Patrick Appleford

1. O Lord, all the world belongs to you,
   and you are always making all things new.
   What is wrong you forgive,
   and the new life you give
   is what's turning the world upside down.

2. The world's only loving to its friends,
   but you have brought us love that never ends;
   loving enemies too,
   and this loving with you
   is what's turning the world upside down.

3. This world lives divided and apart.
   You draw us all together and we start,
   in your body, to see
   that in fellowship we
   can be turning the world upside down.

4. The world wants the wealth to live in state,
   but you show us a new way to be great:
   like a servant you came,
   and if we do the same,
   we'll be turning the world upside down.

5. O Lord, all the world belongs to you,
   and you are always making all things new.
   Send your Spirit on all
   in your church, whom you call
   to be turning the world upside down.

209 Taizé Community

O Lord, hear my prayer,
O Lord, hear my prayer,
when I call, answer me.
O Lord, hear my prayer,
O Lord, hear my prayer,
come and listen to me.

210 Karl Boberg, trans. Stuart K. Hine

1. O Lord, my God, when I, in awesome wonder,
   consider all the works thy hand has made,
   I see the stars, I hear the rolling thunder,
   thy pow'r throughout the universe displayed.

   Then sings my soul, my Saviour God, to thee:
   how great thou art, how great thou art.
   Then sings my soul, my Saviour God, to thee:
   how great thou art, how great thou art.

2. When through the woods and forest glades I wander
   and hear the birds sing sweetly in the trees;
   when I look down from lofty mountain grandeur,
   and hear the brook, and feel the gentle breeze.

3. And when I think that God, his Son not sparing,
   sent him to die, I scarce can take it in
   that on the cross, my burden gladly bearing,
   he bled and died to take away my sin.

4. When Christ shall come with shout of acclamation
   and take me home, what joy shall fill my heart;
   when I shall bow in humble adoration,
   and there proclaim: my God, how great thou art.

211 Psalm 131

O Lord, my heart is not proud,
nor haughty my eyes.
I have not gone after things too great,
nor marvels beyond me.
Truly I have set my soul
in silence and peace;
at rest, as a child in it's mother's arms,
so is my soul.

212 Estelle White

1. O my Lord, within my heart
   pride will have no home,
   every talent that I have
   comes from you alone.

   And like a child at rest
   close to its mother's breast,
   safe in your arms
   my soul is calmed.

2. Lord, my eyes do not look high
   nor my thoughts take wings,
   I can find such treasures
   in ordinary things.

3. Great affairs are not for me,
   deeds beyond my scope.
   In the simple things I do
   I find my joy and hope.

213 Damian Lundy

1. One cold night in spring the wind blew strong;
   then the darkness had its hour.
   A man was eating with his friends,
   for he knew his death was near.

2. And he broke a wheaten loaf to share,
   for his friends a last goodbye.
   'My body is the bread I break.
   O, my heart will break and die.'

3. Then he poured good wine into a cup,
   blessed it gently, passed it around.
   'This cup is brimming with my blood.
   Soon the drops will stain the ground.'

4. See a dying man with arms outstretched
   at the setting of the sun.
   He stretches healing hands to you.
   Will you take them for your own?

5. Soon a man will come with arms outstretched
   at the rising of the sun.
   His wounded hands will set you free
   if you take them for your own.

214 Michael Forster

One hundred and fifty-three!
One hundred and fifty-three!
The number of all the fish in the sea:
one hundred and fifty-three!

1. We'd fished all the night for nothing,
   but Jesus said, 'Try once more.'
   So we doubtfully tried
   on the other side
   and found there were fish galore!

2. We got all the fish to the shore,
   we wondered how many there'd be.
   So we started to count,
   and what an amount:
   one hundred and fifty-three!

3. Now here was a wonderful sight
   we'd never expected to see;
   and the net didn't break,
   it was able to take
   the hundred and fifty-three!

4. So whether you're rich or you're poor,
   whatever your race or your sect,
   be you black, white or brown,
   Jesus wants you around,
   there's plenty of room in the net!

215 Sydney Carter

1. One more step along the world I go,
   one more step along the world I go.
   From the old things to the new
   keep me travelling along with you.

   And it's from the old I travel to the new,
   keep me travelling along with you.

2. Round the corners of the world I turn
   more and more about the world I learn.
   All the new things that I see
   you'll be looking at along with me.

3. As I travel through the bad and good,
   keep me travelling the way I should.
   Where I see no way to go
   you'll be telling me the way, I know.

4. Give me courage when the world is rough,
   keep me loving though the world is tough.
   Leap and sing in all I do,
   keep me travelling along with you.

5. You are older than the world can be,
   you are younger than the life in me.
   Ever old and ever new,
   keep me travelling along with you.

1. On our school your blessing, Lord,
   on our school your grace bestow.
   On our school your blessing, Lord,
   may it come and never go.
   Bringing peace and joy and happiness,
   bringing love that knows no end.
   On our school your blessing, Lord,
   on our school your blessing send.

2. On our school your loving, Lord,
   may it overflow each day.
   On our school your loving, Lord,
   may it come and with us stay.
   Drawing us in love and unity
   by the love received from you.
   On our school your loving, Lord,
   may it come each day anew.

3. On our school your giving, Lord,
   may it turn and ever flow.
   On our school your giving, Lord,
   on our school your wealth bestow.
   Filling all our hopes and wishes, lord,
   in the way you know best.
   On our school your giving, Lord,
   may it come and with us rest.

4. On our school your calling, Lord,
   may it come to us each day.
   On our school your calling, Lord,
   may it come to lead the way.

Filling us with nobler yearnings, Lord,
calling us to live in you.
On our school your calling, Lord,
may it come each day anew.

217 Robert Cull

Open our eyes, Lord,
we want to see Jesus,
to reach out and touch him
and say that we love him;
Open our ears, Lord,
and help us to listen;
O open our eyes, Lord,
we want to see Jesus!

218 Estelle White

1. O, the love of my Lord is the essence
   of all that I love here on earth.
   All the beauty I see he has given to me,
   and his giving is gentle as silence.

2. Every day, every hour, every moment
   have been blessed by the strength of his love.
   At the turn of each tide he is there at my side,
   and his touch is as gentle as silence.

3. There've been times when I've turned from his presence,
   and I've walked other paths, other ways;
   but I've called on his name in the dark of my shame,
   and his mercy was gentle as silence.

219 Damian Lundy

O the word of my Lord,
deep within my being,
O the word of my Lord,
you have filled my mind.

1. Before I formed you in the womb
   I knew you through and through,
   I chose you to be mine.
   Before you left your mother's side
   I called to you, my child, to be my sign.

2. I know that you are very young,
   but I will make you strong,
   I'll fill you with my word;
   and you will travel through the land,
   fulfilling my command which you have heard.

3. And everywhere you are to go
   my hand will follow you;
   you will not be alone.
   In all the danger that you fear
   you'll find me very near, your words my own.

4. With all my strength you will be filled:
   you will destroy and build,
   for that is my design.
   You will create and overthrow,
   reap harvests I will sow, your word is mine.

1. Our Father, who art in heaven,
   hallowèd be thy name.
   Thy kingdom come, thy will be done,
   hallowèd be thy name,
   hallowèd be thy name.

2. On earth as it is in heaven,
   hallowèd be thy name.
   Give us this day our daily bread,
   hallowèd be thy name,
   hallowèd be thy name.

3. Forgive us our trespasses,
   hallowèd be thy name.
   As we forgive those who trespass against us,
   hallowèd be thy name,
   hallowèd be thy name.

4. Lead us not into temptation,
   hallowèd be thy name.
   But deliver us from all that is evil,
   hallowèd be thy name,
   hallowèd be thy name.

5. For thine is the kingdom, the pow'r and the glory,
   hallowèd be thy name.
   For ever and for ever and ever,
   hallowèd be thy name,
   hallowèd be thy name.

Continued overleaf

6. Amen, amen, it shall be so,
   hallowèd be thy name.
   Amen, amen, it shall be so,
   hallowèd be thy name,
   hallowèd be thy name.

221 The Lord's Prayer

Our Father, who art in heaven,
hallowed be thy name;
thy kingdom come,
thy will be done on earth as it is in heav'n.
Give us this day our daily bread,
and forgive us our trespasses
as we forgive those who trespass against us;
and lead us not into temptation,
but deliver us from all that is evil.
For the kingdom, the pow'r
and the glory are yours
now and for ever. Amen.

222 Unknown

Our God is so great,
so strong and so mighty,
there's nothing that he cannot do.
Our God is so great,
so strong and so mighty,
there's nothing that he cannot do.

The rivers are his,
the mountains are his,
the stars are his handiwork too.
Our God is so great,
so strong and so mighty,
there's nothing that he cannot do.

223 Michael Forster

Out to the great wide world we go! (3)
and we sing of the love of Jesus.

1. Go and tell our neighbours,
   go and tell our friends,
   Jesus gives his people
   love that never ends. So:

2. People sad and lonely,
   wond'ring how to cope;
   let's find ways of showing
   Jesus gives us hope. So:

224 Ruth Brown

Over the earth is a mat of green,
over the green is dew,
over the dew are the arching trees,
over the trees the blue.
Across the blue are scudding clouds,
over the clouds the sun,
over it all is the love of God,
blessing us every one.

225 Traditional

1. O when the saints go marching in,
   O when the saints go marching in,
   I want to be in that number
   when the saints go marching in.

2. O when they crown him Lord of all . . .

3. O when all knees bow at his name . . .

4. O when they sing the Saviour's praise . . .

5. O when the saints go marching in . . .

226 Peter Madden

Peace I leave with you, peace I give to you;
not as the world gives peace, do I give.
Take and pass it on, on to everyone:
thus the world will know, you are my friends.

© 1976 Kevin Mayhew Ltd.

227 Unknown

1. Peace is flowing like a river,
   flowing out through you and me,
   spreading out into the desert,
   setting all the captives free.

   Let it flow through me,
   let it flow through me,
   let the mighty peace of God
   flow out through me.
   (Repeat)

2. Love is flowing like a river . . .

3. Joy is flowing like a river . . .

4. Faith is flowing like a river . . .

5. Hope is flowing like a river . . .

228 Kevin Mayhew

1. Peace, perfect peace,
   is the gift of Christ our Lord.
   Peace, perfect peace,
   is the gift of Christ our Lord.
   Thus, says the Lord,
   will the world know my friends.
   Peace, perfect peace,
   is the gift of Christ our Lord.

2. Love, perfect love . . .

3. Faith, perfect faith . . .

4. Hope, perfect hope . . .

5. Joy, perfect joy . . .

© 1976 Kevin Mayhew Ltd.

229 Unknown

Praise and thanksgiving let everyone bring
unto our Father for every good thing!
All together joyfully sing.

230 Thomas Ken

Praise God from whom all blessings flow,
praise him, all creatures here below;
praise him above, ye heav'nly host,
praise Father, Son and Holy Ghost.

231 Michael Forster

1. Praise God in his holy place!
   He's the God of time and space.
   Praise him, all the human race!
   Let everything praise our God!

2. Praise him with the ol' wood block!
   Let it swing and let it rock,
   praising God around the clock!
   Let everything praise our God!

3. Praise him with the big bass drum,
   if you've got guitars, then strum!
   Now let's make those rafters hum!
   Let everything praise our God!

4. Praise him with the chime bars' chime,
   tell the bells it's party time,
   help those singers find a rhyme!
   Let everything praise our God!

5. Violin or xylophone,
   trumpets with their awesome tone;
   bowed or beaten, bashed or blown,
   Let everything praise our God!

6. Cymbals, triangles and things,
   if it crashes, howls or rings,
   everybody shout and sing!
   Let everything praise our God!

232 Unknown

1. Praise him, praise him,
   praise him in the morning,
   praise him in the noontime.
   Praise him, praise him,
   praise him when the sun goes down.

2. Love him, love him . . .

3. Trust him, trust him . . .

4. Serve him, serve him . . .

5. Jesus, Jesus . . .

233 Mike Anderson

Praise the Lord, all of you peoples!
Praise the Lord, shout for joy!
Praise the Lord, sing him a new song!
Praise the Lord and bless his name.

1. Clap your hands, now, all of you nations.
   Shout for joy! Acclaim the Lord.

2. God goes up to shouts which acclaim him,
   God goes up to trumpet blast.

3. Let the music sound for our Saviour,
   let each chord resound in praise.

Continued overleaf

4. He is King of all the nations;
   honour him by singing psalms.

   Praise the Lord, all of you peoples!
   Praise the Lord, shout for joy!
   Praise the Lord, sing him a new song!
   Praise the Lord and bless his name.

234 The Missal

Praise to you, O Christ,
King of eternal glory.
Praise to you, O Christ,
King of eternal glory!

235 Susan Sayers

Push, little seed,
push, push, little seed,
till your head pops out of the ground.
This is the air,
and now you are there
you can have a good look round.
You'll see God's sky,
you'll see God's sun,
you'll feel his raindrops one by one,
as you grow, grow, grow, grow,
grow to be wheat for bread.
So push, little seed,
push, push, little seed,
that the world may be fed.

236 Estelle White

1. Put your trust in the man who tamed the sea,
   put your trust in the man who calmed the waves,
   put your trust in the Lord Jesus,
   it is he who rescues and saves.

2. Put your trust in the man who cured the blind,
   put your trust in the man who helped the lame,
   put your trust in the Lord Jesus,
   there is healing strength in his name.

3. Put your trust in the man who died for you,
   put your trust in the man who conquered fear,
   put your trust in the Lord Jesus,
   for he rose from death and he's near.

4. Put your trust in the man who understands,
   put your trust in the man who is your friend,
   put your trust in the Lord Jesus,
   who will give you life without end.

237 Evelyn Tarner

Rejoice in the Lord always,
and again I say rejoice.
Rejoice in the Lord always,
and again I say rejoice.
Rejoice, rejoice,
and again I say rejoice.
Rejoice, rejoice,
and again I say rejoice.

Rise and shine, and give God his glory, glory.
Rise and shine, and give God his glory, glory.
Rise and shine, and give God his glory, glory,
children of the Lord.

1. The Lord said to Noah, 'There's gonna be a
       floody, floody.'
   Lord said to Noah, 'There's gonna be a
       floody, floody.'
   Get those children out of the muddy, muddy,
   children of the Lord.

2. So Noah, he built him, he built him an arky, arky,
   Noah, he built him, he built him an arky, arky,
   built it out of hickory barky, barky,
   children of the Lord.

3. The animals, they came on, they came on, by
       twosies, twosies,
   animals, they came on, they came on, by
       twosies, twosies,
   elephants and kangaroosies, roosies,
   children of the Lord.

4. It rained and poured for forty daysies, daysies,
   rained and poured for forty daysies, daysies,
   nearly drove those animals crazyies, crazyies,
   children of the Lord.

5. The sun came out and dried up the landy, landy,
   sun came out and dried up the landy, landy,
   everything was fine and dandy, dandy,
   children of the Lord.

6. If you get to heaven before I do-sies, do-sies,
   you get to heaven before I do-sies, do-sies,
   tell those angels I'm coming too-sies, too-sies,
   children of the Lord.

239 Sydney Carter

1. Said Judas to Mary, 'Now what will you do
   with your ointment so rich and so rare?'
   'I'll pour it all over the feet of the Lord,
   and I'll wipe it away with my hair,' she said,
   'I'll wipe it away with my hair.'

2. 'Oh Mary, oh Mary, oh think of the poor,
   this ointment, it could have been sold,
   and think of the blankets and think of the bread
   you could buy with the silver and gold,' he said,
   'you could buy with the silver and gold.'

3. 'Tomorrow, tomorrow I'll think of the poor,
   tomorrow,' she said, 'not today;
   for dearer than all of the poor in the world
   is my love who is going away,' she said,
   'is my love who is going away.'

4. Said Jesus to Mary, 'Your love is so deep,
   today you may do as you will.
   Tomorrow you say I am going away,
   but my body I leave with you still,' he said,
   'my body I leave with you still.'

5. 'The poor of the world are my body,' he said,
   'to the end of the world they shall be.
   The bread and the blankets you give to the poor
   you'll know you have given to me,' he said,
   'you'll know you have given to me.'

Continued overleaf

6. 'My body will hang on the cross of the world,
   tomorrow,' he said, 'and today,
   and Martha and Mary will find me again
   and wash all my sorrow away,' he said,
   'and wash all my sorrow away.'

240   Kevin Mayhew, based on the Office of Compline

Save us, O Lord, while we are awake,
and guard us while we sleep,
that awake we may watch with Christ,
and asleep we may rest in peace,
in Jesus' name,
in Jesus' name.

241   Karen Lafferty

1. Seek ye first the kingdom of God
   and his righteousness,
   and all these things shall be added unto you;
   allelu, alleluia!

   Alleluia, alleluia,
   Alleluia, allelu, alleluia,

2. You shall not live by bread alone,
   but by every word
   that proceeds from the mouth of God;
   allelu, alleluia!

3. Ask and it shall be given unto you,
   seek and you shall find;
   knock and it shall be opened unto you;
   allelu, alleluia!

242 Aniceto Nazareth

Send forth your Spirit, O Lord,
that the face of the earth be renewed.

1. O my soul, arise and bless the Lord God.
   Say to him: 'My God, how great you are.
   You are clothed with majesty and splendour,
   and light is the garment you wear.'

2. 'You have built your palace on the waters.
   Like the winds, the angels do your word.
   You have set the earth on its foundations,
   so firm, to be shaken no more.'

3. 'All your creatures look to you for comfort;
   from your open hand they have their fill.
   You send forth your Spirit and revive them,
   the face of the earth you renew.'

4. While I live, I sing the Lord God's praises;
   I will thank the author of those marvels.
   Praise to God, the Father, Son and Spirit
   both now and for ever. Amen.

243 Kontakion (Eastern Orthodox Liturgy)

Set my heart on fire with love for you,
O Christ my God, that in its flame
I may love you with all my heart,
with all my soul, with all my strength,
and my neighbour as myself,
so that keeping your commandments
I may glorify you,
the giver of all good gifts,
so that keeping your commandments
I may glorify you,
the giver of all good gifts.

244 Sandra Joan Billington

Shalom, my friend,
shalom, my friend,
shalom, shalom.
The peace of Christ I give you today,
shalom, shalom.

245 Unknown

1. Sing alleluia.
   Sing alleluia.
   Sing alleluia.
   You are my Lord.

2. Father, I thank you.
   Father, I thank you.
   Father, I thank you.
   You are my Lord.

3. Jesus, I love you.
   Jesus, I love you.
   Jesus, I love you.
   You are my Lord.

4. Spirit, I need you.
   Spirit, I need you.
   Spirit, I need you.
   You are my Lord.

5. Sing alleluia.
   Sing alleluia.
   Sing alleluia.
   You are my Lord.

246 Carey Landry

1. Sing a simple song unto the Lord,
   sing a simple song unto the Lord,
   sing it with your heart, sing it with your soul,
   sing a simple song unto the Lord.

   Oh Lord, I love you,
   Oh Lord, I see.
   Oh Lord, I love you,
   I see that you love me.

2. Say a simple prayer unto the Lord,
   say a simple prayer unto the Lord,
   say it with your heart, say it with your soul,
   say a simple prayer unto the Lord.

3. Give a simple gift unto the Lord,
   give a simple gift unto the Lord,
   give it with your heart, give it with your soul,
   give a simple gift unto the Lord.

247 Michael Forster

Sing, holy mother,
bringing hope to birth,
with the poor and humble
sing of human worth.

1. Blessed are you among women,
   full of mysterious grace;
   holding the hopes of creation
   in your maternal embrace.

2. Stand with the lost and the lonely,
   those whom the vain world denies,
   join with the weak and the foolish,
   humbling the strong and the wise!

3. Sing of the values of heaven,
   shame our respectable pride!
   Sing to the spurned and the fearful,
   tell them no longer to hide!

248 Mike Anderson

Sing it in the valleys,
shout it from the mountain tops:
Jesus came to save us,
and his saving never stops.
He is King of kings,
and new life he brings.
Sing it in the valleys,
shout it from the mountain tops.
Oh, shout it from the mountain tops.

1. Jesus, you are by my side,
   you take all my fears.
   If I only come to you,
   you will heal the pain of years.

2. You have not deserted me,
   though I go astray.
   Jesus, take me in your arms,
   help me walk with you today.

3. Jesus, you are living now,
   Jesus, I believe.
   Jesus, take me, heart and soul.
   Yours alone I want to be.

© Mike Anderson

249 Michael Forster

1. Sing out in joy to the God of all creation,
   who made the world and put it in a spin.
   Our life revolves round the God of all creation:
   he speaks, and whole new galaxies begin.

   Praise our God who is great but is also small,
   who has looked at the world from a cattle stall,
   and who sits in the dust where his people fall,
   when he lifts us up and tells us that he loves us all.

2. Sing out in joy to the God of liberation,
   who leads us all to hope and liberty.
   We'll journey on with the God of liberation,
   proclaim his truth and set his people free.

Continued overleaf

3. Sing out in joy to the God of our salvation,
   who calls us friends and fills us with his grace.
   Death is destroyed by the God of our salvation,
   who gives us life abundant in its place.

   Praise our God who is great but is also small,
   who has looked at the world from a cattle stall,
   and who sits in the dust where his people fall,
   when he lifts us up and tells us that he loves us all.

4. Sing out in joy to the God of all creation,
   Whose glory sets a billion stars ablaze.
   Sing out in joy to the God of all creation,
   let every atom ring with glorious praise.

250 W. L. Wallace

1. Sing praise to God, sing praise to God for life,
   for beauty, hope and love, for tenderness and grace.
   Sing praise to God, sing praise to God for life,
   with all of earth, sing and praise all God's life.

2. Lift up your eyes to see the works of God,
   in every blade of grass, in every human face.
   Lift up your eyes to see the works of God,
   through all of life, in all time and all space.

3. Open your ears to hear the cries of pain
   arising from the poor and all who are oppressed.
   Open your mind and use your wits to find
   who are the cause of this world's unjust ways.

4. Reach out your hands to share the wealth God gave
   with those who are oppressed, and those who feel
      alone.
   Reach out your hands and gently touch with Christ
   each frozen heart which has said 'No' to love.

5. Open our hearts to love the world with Christ,
   each person in this world, each creature of this earth.
   Open our hearts to love the ones who hate,
   and in their hearts find a part of ourselves.

6. Live life with love, for love encircles all;
   it casts out all our fears, it fills the heart with joy.
   Live life with love, for love transforms our life,
   as we praise God with our eyes, hands and hearts.

251 Bob Dufford

Sing to the mountains, sing to the sea,
raise your voices, lift your hearts.
This is the day the Lord has made,
let all the earth rejoice.

1. I will give thanks to you, my Lord,
   you have answered my plea;
   you have saved my soul from death,
   you are my strength and my song.

2. Holy, holy, holy Lord,
   heaven and earth are full of your glory.

3. This is the day that the Lord has made,
   let us be glad and rejoice.
   He has turned all death to life,
   sing of the glory of God.

252 Richard Farrow

Stand on the corner of the street,
listen for God's heartbeat:
you can hear it in the chatter,
in the bustle and the clatter
and the patter of the people's feet.

1. God is living everywhere,
   he's found in every place:
   in crowded squares and shopping streets
   you'll always see his face.

2. God is living everywhere
   that human life is found.
   In cafés, shops and car parks, too,
   his Spirit is around.

3. God is living everywhere,
   in all the human race,
   in schools and flats and offices,
   in everybody's face.

253 Taizé Community

Stay with me,
remain here with me,
watch and pray,
watch and pray.

254 Gill Hutchinson

Step by step, on and on,
we will walk with Jesus till the journey's done.
Step by step, day by day,
because Jesus is the living way.

1. He's the one to follow,
   in his footsteps we will tread.
   Don't worry about tomorrow,
   Jesus knows the way ahead. Oh,

2. He will never leave us,
   And his love he'll always show,
   so wherever Jesus leads us,
   that's the way we want to go. Oh,

© 1994 Sea Dream Music

255 Christine McCann

Take and bless our gifts,
take and bless our gifts,
take and bless our gifts,
take and bless them, Lord.
(Repeat)

1. Blessed are you, Lord, God of all creation.
   Through your goodness we offer you this bread,
   which earth has given and human hands have made.
   It will become for us the bread of life.

2. Blessed are you, Lord, God of all creation.
   Through your goodness we offer you this wine,
   fruit of the vine and work of human hands.
   It will become for us the wine of life.

Continued overleaf

3. Blessed are you, Lord, God of all creation.
   Through your goodness we offer you our lives.
   Accept and sanctify all we try to do,
   for the praise and glory of your name.

256 Francesca Leftley

1. Take me, Lord, use my life in the way you wish to do.
   Fill me, Lord, touch my heart till it always thinks of you.
   Take me now, as I am, this is all I can offer.

   Here today I, the clay,
   will be moulded by my Lord.

2. Lord, I pray that each day I will listen to your will.
   Many times I have failed but I know you love me still.
   Teach me now, guide me, Lord, keep me close to
       you always.

3. I am weak, fill me now with your strength and set
       me free.
   Make me whole, fashion me so that you will live
       in me.
   Hold me now in your hands, form me now with
       your Spirit.

257 Sebastian Temple

1. Take my hands and make them as your own,
   and use them for your kingdom here on earth.
   Consecrate them to your care,
   anoint them for your service
   where you may need your gospel to be sown.

2. Take my hands, they speak now for my heart,
   and by their actions they will show their love.
   Guard them on their daily course,
   be their strength and guiding force,
   to ever serve the Trinity above.

3. Take my hands, I give them to you, Lord.
   Prepare them for the service of your name.
   Open them to human need
   and by their love they'll sow your seed
   so all may know the love and hope you give.

258 Joe Wise

Take our bread, we ask you,
take our hearts, we love you,
take our lives, O Father,
we are yours, we are yours.

1. Yours as we stand at the table you set,
   yours as we eat the bread our hearts can't forget.
   We are the signs of your life with us yet;
   we are yours, we are yours.

2. Your holy people stand washed in your blood,
   Spirit-filled, yet hungry, we await your food.
   Poor though we are, we have brought ourselves
       to you:
   we are yours, we are yours.

259 Jean Holloway

Thanks for the fellowship found at this meal,
thanks for a day refreshed;
thanks to the Lord for his presence we feel,
thanks for the food he blessed.
Joyfully sing praise to the Lord,
praise to the risen Son.
Alleluia, ever-adored,
pray that his will be done.
As he was known in the breaking of bread,
now he is known again;
and by his hand have the hungry been fed,
thanks be to Christ. Amen!

260 Susan Sayers

1. Thank you for the summer morning,
   misting into heat;
   thank you for the diamonds
   of dew beneath my feet;
   thank you for the silver
   where a snail has wandered by;
   oh, we praise the name
   of him who made
   the earth and sea and sky.

2. Thank you for the yellow fields
   of corn like waving hair;
   thank you for the red surprise
   of poppies here and there;

thank you for the blue of
an electric dragonfly;
oh, we praise the name
of him who made
the earth and sea and sky.

3. Thank you for the splintered light
among the brooding trees;
thank you for the leaves that rustle
in a sudden breeze;
thank you for the branches
and the fun of climbing high;
oh, we praise the name
of him who made
the earth and sea and sky.

4. Thank you for the evening
as the light begins to fade;
clouds so red and purple
that the setting sun has made;
thank you for the shadows
as the owls come gliding by;
oh, we praise the name
of him who made
the earth and sea and sky.

261 Diane Davis Andrew, adapted by Geoffrey Marshall-Taylor

1. Thank you, Lord, for this new day, (3)
right where we are.

    *Alleluia, praise the Lord, (3)
    right where we are.*

Continued overleaf

2. Thank you, Lord, for food to eat, (3)
   right where we are.

   Alleluia, praise the Lord, (3)
   right where we are.

3. Thank you, Lord, for clothes to wear, (3)
   right where we are.

4. Thank you, Lord, for all your gifts, (3)
   right where we are.

262 Sydney Carter

1. The bell of creation is swinging for ever
   in all of the things that are coming to be,
   the bell of creation is swinging for ever
   and all of the while it is swinging in me.

   Swing, bell, over the land!
   Swing, bell, under the sea!
   The bell of creation is swinging for ever
   and all of the while it is swinging in me.

2. In all of my loving, in all of my labour,
   in all of the things that are coming to be,
   in all of my loving, in all of my labour,
   the bell of creation is swinging in me.

3. I look to the life that is living for ever
   in all of the things that are coming to be,
   I look to the life that is living for ever
   and all of the while it is looking for me.

4. I'll swing with the bell that is swinging for ever,
   in all of the things that are coming to be,
   I'll swing with the bell that is swinging for ever,
   and all of the while it is swinging in me.

263 Susan Sayers

The clock tells the story of time God gave us,
measured in a tick-tock way.
Don't waste a second of the time God gave us;
all too soon it flies away.

1. Driving lorries, licking lollies,
   pushing heavy trolleys
   round the supermarket store;
   washing faces, tying laces,
   blinking, winking, drinking
   and much more you can be sure.

2. Time is good for thinking in,
   for helping other people in,
   or playing with a friend;
   time is like a funny kind of
   pocket money given
   every day for us to spend.

264 B. C. Hanson

1. The duck goes 'Quack'. (2)
   It swings across the yard and back.
   The duck goes 'Quack'. (2)
   I'm glad that God made ducks.

Continued overleaf

2. The cow goes 'Moo'. (2)
   She gives good milk to me and you.
   The cow goes 'Moo'. (2)
   I'm glad that God made cows.

3. The horse goes 'Neigh'. (2)
   It likes to run and eat good hay.
   The horse goes 'Neigh'. (2)
   I'm glad God made the horse.

4. The cat goes 'Purr'. (2)
   I like to pet her soft warm fur.
   The cat goes 'Purr'. (2)
   I'm glad that God made cats.

5. The dog can bark. (2)
   It likes to run around the park.
   The dog can bark. (2)
   I'm glad that God made dogs.

265 Mike Anderson

The kingdom (the kingdom)
of heaven (of heaven),
the kingdom of heaven is yours.
A new world (a new world)
in Jesus (in Jesus),
a new world in Jesus is yours.

1. Blessed are you in sorrow and grief:
   for you shall all be consoled.
   Blessed are you the gentle in heart:
   you shall inherit the earth.

2. Blessed are you who hunger for right:
   for you shall be satisfied.
   Blessed are you the merciful ones:
   for you shall be pardoned too.

3. Blessed are you whose hearts are pure:
   your eyes shall gaze on the Lord.
   Blessed are you who strive after peace:
   the Lord will call you his own.

4. Blessed are you who suffer for right:
   the heavenly kingdom is yours.
   Blessed are you who suffer for me:
   for you shall reap your reward.

© Mike Anderson

266 Graham Kendrick

1. The King is among us,
   his Spirit is here,
   let's draw near and worship,
   let songs fill the air.

2. He looks down upon us,
   delight in his face,
   enjoying his children's love,
   enthralled by our praise.

3. For each child is special,
   accepted and loved,
   a love-gift from Jesus
   to his Father above.

Continued overleaf

4. And now he is giving
   his gifts to us all,
   for no one is worthless
   and each one is called.

5. The Spirit's anointing
   on all flesh comes down,
   and we shall be channels
   for works like his own.

6. We come now believing
   your promise of pow'r,
   for we are your people
   and this is your hour.

7. The King is among us,
   his Spirit is here,
   let's draw near and worship,
   let songs fill the air.

© 1981 Kingsway's Thankyou Music

267 Willard F. Jabusch

The King of glory comes,
the nation rejoices,
open the gates before him,
lift up your voices.

1. Who is the King of glory,
   how shall we call him?
   He is Emmanuel,
   the promised of ages.

2. In all of Galilee,
   in city and village,
   he goes among his people,
   curing their illness.

3. Sing then of David's Son,
   our Saviour and brother,
   in all of Galilee
   was never another.

4. He gave his life for us,
   the pledge of salvation.
   He took upon himself
   the sins of the nation.

5. He conquered sin and death;
   he truly has risen;
   and he will share with us
   his heavenly vision.

268 John Foley

The Lord hears the cry of the poor.
Blessed be the Lord.

1. I will bless the Lord at all times,
   his praise ever in my mouth.
   Let my soul glory in the Lord,
   for he hears the cry of the poor.

Continued overleaf

2. Let the lowly hear and be glad:
   the Lord listens to their pleas;
   and to hearts broken he is near,
   for he hears the cry of the poor.

   The Lord hears the cry of the poor.
   Blessed be the Lord.

3. Every spirit crushed he will save;
   will be ransom for their lives;
   will be safe shelter for their fears,
   for he hears the cry of the poor.

4. We proclaim the greatness of God,
   his praise ever in our mouth;
   every face brightened in his light,
   for he hears the cry of the poor.

269 Jean-Paul Lécot, trans. W. R. Lawrence

1. The Lord is alive! Alleluia!
   He dwells in our midst! Alleluia!
   Give praise to his name
   throughout all the world!
   Alleluia! Alleluia!

2. He brings us great joy! Alleluia!
   He fills us with hope! Alleluia!
   He comes as our food,
   he gives us our life!
   Alleluia! Alleluia!

3. So let us rejoice! Alleluia!
   Give praise to the Lord! Alleluia!
   He showed us his love,
   by him we are saved!
   Alleluia! Alleluia!

4. The Lord is alive! Alleluia!
   So let us proclaim, alleluia,
   the Good News of Christ
   throughout all the world!
   Alleluia! Alleluia!

5. Christ Jesus has died! Alleluia!
   Christ Jesus is ris'n! Alleluia!
   Christ Jesus will come
   again as Lord!
   Alleluia! Alleluia!

6. Sing praises to God, alleluia,
   who reigns without end! Alleluia!
   The Father, the Son,
   and Spirit – all One!
   Alleluia! Alleluia!

270 Gail Cole

1. The Lord is present in his sanctuary,
   let us praise the Lord.
   The Lord is present in his people gathered here,
   let us praise the Lord.
   Praise him, praise him,
   let us praise the Lord.
   Praise him, praise him,
   let us praise Jesus!

Continued overleaf

2. The Lord is present in his sanctuary,
   let us sing to the Lord.
   The Lord is present in his people gathered here,
   let us sing to the Lord.
   Sing to him, sing to him,
   let us sing to the Lord.
   Sing to him, sing to him,
   let us sing to Jesus!

3. The Lord is present in his sanctuary,
   let us love the Lord.
   The Lord is present in his people gathered here,
   let us love the Lord.
   Love him, love him,
   let us love the Lord.
   Love him, love him,
   let us love the Lord.

271 John Gowans

1. There are hundreds of sparrows, thousands, millions,
   they're two a penny, far too many there must be;
   there are hundreds and thousands, millions of
        sparrows,
   but God knows every one, and God knows me.

2. There are hundreds of flowers, thousands, millions,
   and flowers fair the meadows wear for all to see;
   there are hundreds and thousands, millions of
        flowers,
   but God knows every one, and God knows me.

3. There are hundreds of planets, thousands, millions,
   way out in space each has a place by God's decree;
   there are hundreds and thousands, millions of planets,
   but God knows every one, and God knows me.

4. There are hundreds of children, thousands, millions,
   and yet their names are written on God's memory;
   there are hundreds and thousands, millions of
      children,
   but God knows every one, and God knows me.

272   Dave Davidson

1. There are people who live in mansions,
   there are people who live in flats,
   there are people who live on open streets
   and God's not pleased with that!

   Gotta put the world to rights!
   Gotta put the world to rights!
   Gotta put the world to rights! God help us!
   Gotta put the world to rights!

2. There are people who feed on salmon,
   there are people who feed on stew,
   there are people who hardly feed at all,
   and God says that won't do!

3. There are people with famous faces,
   there are people with famous names,
   there are people whom no one knows at all,
   and God says that's a shame.

273 Cecil Frances Alexander, alt.

1. There is a green hill far away,
   outside a city wall,
   where Christ our Lord was crucified,
   who died to save us all.

2. We may not know, we cannot tell,
   what pains he had to bear,
   but we believe it was for us
   he hung and suffered there.

3. He died that we might be forgiv'n,
   that God might call us good,
   that we might go at last to heav'n,
   saved by his precious blood.

4. O dearly, dearly has he loved,
   so let us love him too,
   and trust in his redeeming blood,
   and try his works to do.

274 Melody Green

1. There is a Redeemer,
   Jesus, God's own Son,
   precious Lamb of God, Messiah,
   Holy One.

   Thank you, O my Father,
   for giving us your Son,
   and leaving your Spirit
   till the work on earth is done.

2. Jesus, my Redeemer,
   Name above all names,
   precious Lamb of God, Messiah,
   O for sinners slain.

3. When I stand in glory
   I will see his face.
   And there I'll serve my King for ever,
   in that holy place.

275 Michael Forster

There's a great big world out there. Let's go!
There's a great big world out there. Let's go!
There's a great big world out there. Let's go!
Celebrate the love of God!

1. We've sung about the love of God,
   now it's time to let it show.
   If we don't act as though it's true,
   how on earth will people know?

2. We've brought to God our prayers and hymns,
   now it's time to live his life,
   to sow a little love and peace
   in the place of selfish strife.

3. We've listened to the word of God,
   now it's time to live it out,
   to show by everything we do
   what the gospel is about.

276 Michael Forster

There's a rainbow in the sky, and it's okay! (3)
It's a sign that God is good.

1. Forty days and nights afloat,
   all cooped up on Noah's boat!
   Now the rain is almost done;
   wake up world, here comes the sun!

2. Now we've got another start,
   everyone can play a part:
   make the world a better place,
   put a smile on every face!

3. Sometimes, still, the world is bad,
   people hungry, people sad.
   Jesus wants us all to care,
   showing people everywhere:

277 Susan Sayers

1. There's a seed in a flow'r
   on a plant in a garden
   of the world, as it swirls
   through the wideness of space . . .

   of our star-speckled galaxy,
   speck of the universe,
   made and sustained
   by the love of our God.

2. There's an ant in a nest
   on the floor of a forest
   of the world, as it swirls
   through the wideness of space . . .

3. There's a crab in a shell
   in the depth of an ocean
   of the world, as it swirls
   through the wideness of space . . .

4. There's a child in a school
   of a town in a country
   of the world, as it swirls
   through the wideness of space . . .

278 Christina Wilde

There was one, there were two,
there were three friends of Jesus,
there were four, there were five,
there were six friends of Jesus,
there were sev'n, there were eight,
there were nine friends of Jesus,
ten friends of Jesus in the band.

1. Bells are going to ring in praise of Jesus,
   praise of Jesus, praise of Jesus,
   bells are going to ring in praise of Jesus,
   praising Jesus the Lord.

2. Drums are going to boom in praise of Jesus,
   praise of Jesus, praise of Jesus,
   drums are going to boom in praise of Jesus,
   praising Jesus the Lord.

Continued overleaf

3. Tambourines will shake in praise of Jesus,
   praise of Jesus, praise of Jesus,
   tambourines will shake in praise of Jesus,
   praising Jesus the Lord.

   There was one, there were two,
   there were three friends of Jesus,
   there were four, there were five,
   there were six friends of Jesus,
   there were sev'n, there were eight,
   there were nine friends of Jesus,
   ten friends of Jesus in the band.

4. Trumpets will resound in praise of Jesus,
   praise of Jesus, praise of Jesus,
   trumpets will resound in praise of Jesus,
   praising Jesus the Lord.

Verses may be added ad lib, for example:

   Clarinets will swing in praise of Jesus . . .

   Play recorders, too . . .

   Triangles will ting . . .

   Fiddles will be scraped . . .

   Let guitars be strummed . . .

   Chime bars will be chimed . . .

   Glockenspiels will play . . .

   Vibraphones will throb . . .

   Trombones slide about . . .

279 Damian Lundy

1. The Spirit lives to set us free,
   walk, walk in the light.
   He binds us all in unity,
   walk, walk in the light.

   Walk in the light,
   walk in the light,
   walk in the light,
   walk in the light of the Lord.

2. Jesus promised life to all,
   walk, walk in the light.
   The dead were wakened by his call,
   walk, walk in the light.

3. He died in pain on Calvary,
   walk, walk in the light,
   to save the lost like you and me,
   walk, walk in the light.

4. We know his death was not the end,
   walk, walk in the light.
   He gave his Spirit to be our friend,
   walk, walk in the light.

5. By Jesus' love our wounds are healed,
   walk, walk in the light.
   The Father's kindness is revealed,
   walk, walk in the light.

6. The Spirit lives in you and me,
   walk, walk in the light.
   His light will shine for all to see,
   walk, walk in the light.

280 Michael Forster

1. The voice from the bush said: Moses, look snappy,
   have I got a job for you!
   I've looked around and I'm not very happy.
   Here is what you have to do:

   Lead my people to freedom! (3)
   Got to go to the Promised Land!

2. The people of God were suff'ring and dying,
   sick and tired of slavery.
   All God could hear was the sound of their crying;
   Moses had to set them free.

3. We know that the world is still full of sorrow,
   people need to be set free.
   We've got to give them a better tomorrow,
   so God says to you and me:

281 Unknown

1. The wise man built his house upon the rock,
   the wise man built his house upon the rock,
   the wise man built his house upon the rock,
   and the rain came tumbling down.
   And the rain came down and the floods came up,
   the rain came down and the floods came up,
   the rain came down and the floods came up,
   and the house on the rock stood firm.

2. The foolish man built his house upon the sand,
   the foolish man built his house upon the sand,
   the foolish man built his house upon the sand,
   and the rain came tumbling down.
   And the rain came down and the floods came up,
   the rain came down and the floods came up,
   the rain came down and the floods came up,
   and the house on the sand fell flat.

282 Michael Forster

The world is full of smelly feet,
weary from the dusty street.
The world is full of smelly feet,
we'll wash them for each other.

1. Jesus said to his disciples,
   'Wash those weary toes!
   Do it in a cheerful fashion,
   never hold your nose!'

2. People on a dusty journey
   need a place to rest;
   Jesus says, 'You say you love me,
   this will be the test!'

3. We're his friends, we recognise him
   in the folk we meet;
   smart or scruffy, we'll still love him,
   wash his smelly feet.

283 Susan Sayers

1. Think big: an elephant.
   Think bigger: a submarine.
   Think bigger: the highest mountain
   that anyone has ever seen.
   Yet big, big, bigger is God,
   and he loves us all!

2. Think old: a vintage car.
   Think older: a full grown tree.
   Think older: a million grains
   of the sand beside the surging sea.
   Yet old, old, older is God,
   and he loves us all!

3. Think strong: a tiger's jaw.
   Think stronger: a castle wall.
   Think stronger: a hurricane
   that leaves little standing there at all.
   Yet strong, strong, stronger is God,
   and he loves us all!

284 Doreen Newport

1. Think of a world without any flowers,
   think of a world without any trees,
   think of a sky without any sunshine,
   think of the air without any breeze.
   We thank you, Lord, for flow'rs and trees and
       sunshine,
   we thank you, Lord, and praise your holy name.

2. Think of a world without any animals,
   think of a field without any herd,
   think of a stream without any fishes,
   think of a dawn without any bird.
   We thank you, Lord, for all your living creatures,
   we thank you, Lord, and praise your holy name.

3. Think of a world without any people,
   think of a street with no one living there,
   think of a town without any houses,
   no one to love and nobody to care.
   We thank you, Lord, for families and friendships,
   we thank you, Lord, and praise your holy name.

285 vv 1 and 2 Jimmy Owens, vv 3-5 Damian Lundy

1. This is my body, broken for you,
   bringing you wholeness, making you free.
   Take it and eat it, and when you do,
   do it in love for me.

2. This is my blood, poured out for you,
   bringing forgiveness, making you free.
   Take it and drink it, and when you do,
   do it in love for me.

3. Back to my Father soon I shall go.
   Do not forget me; then you will see
   I am still with you, and you will know
   you're very close to me.

4. Filled with my Spirit, how you will grow!
   You are my branches; I am the tree.
   If you are faithful, others will know
   you are alive in me.

Continued overleaf

5. Love one another: I have loved you,
   and I have shown you how to be free;
   serve one another, and when you do,
   do it in love for me.

286 Kevin Mayhew, based on Scripture

This is my command to you:
Love one another,
just as I, the Lord, love you,
love one another.
Amen, so shall it be,
amen, so shall it be.
Amen, so shall it be,
amen, so shall it be.

287 Les Garrett

1. This is the day,
   this is the day that the Lord has made,
   that the Lord has made;
   we will rejoice,
   we will rejoice, and be glad in it,
   and be glad in it.
   This is the day that the Lord has made;
   we will rejoice and be glad in it.
   This is the day,
   this is the day that the Lord has made.

2. This is the day, this is the day
   when he rose again, when he rose again;
   we will rejoice, we will rejoice,
   and be glad in it, and be glad in it.
   This is the day when he rose again;
   we will rejoice and be glad in it.
   This is the day, this is the day
   when he rose again.

3. This is the day, this is the day
   when the Spirit came, when the Spirit came;
   we will rejoice, we will rejoice,
   and be glad in it, and be glad in it.
   This is the day when the Spirit came;
   we will rejoice and be glad in it.
   This is the day, this is the day
   when the Spirit came.

288 Traditional, alt.

*This little light of mine, I'm gonna let it shine, (3)
let it shine, let it shine, let it shine.*

1. The light that shines is the light of love,
   lights the darkness from above,
   it shines on me and it shines on you,
   and shows what the power of love can do.
   I'm gonna shine my light both far and near,
   I'm gonna shine my light both bright and clear.
   Where there's a dark corner in this land,
   I'm gonna let my little light shine.

Continued overleaf

2. On Monday he gave me the gift of love.
   Tuesday peace came from above.
   On Wednesday he told me to have more faith.
   On Thursday he gave me a little more grace.
   Friday he told me just to watch and pray.
   Saturday he told me just what to say.
   On Sunday he gave me the pow'r divine
   to let my little light shine.

   This little light of mine, I'm gonna let it shine, (3)
   let it shine, let it shine, let it shine.

289 Susan Sayers

This world you have made is a beautiful place,
it tells the pow'r of your love.
We rejoice in the beauty of your world,
from the seas to the heavens above.

1. The morning whispers of purity;
   the gathering darkness, peace;
   the waves proclaim your exuberance
   in the awesome pow'r you release.

2. The tenderness of a new-born child,
   the gentleness of the rain,
   simplicity in a single cell,
   and complexity in a brain.

3. Your stillness rests in a silent pool,
   infinity drifts in space;
   your grandeur straddles the mountain tops,
   and we see your face in each face.

290 Dan Schutte

Though the mountains may fall
and the hills turn to dust,
yet the love of the Lord will stand
as a shelter for all
who will call on his name.
Sing the praise and the glory of God.

1. Could the Lord ever leave you?
   Could the Lord forget his love?
   Though the mother forsake her child,
   he will not abandon you.

2. Should you turn and forsake him,
   he will gently call your name.
   Should you wander away from him,
   he will always take you back.

3. Go to him when you're weary;
   he will give you eagle's wings.
   You will run, never tire,
   for your God will be your strength.

4. As he swore to your fathers,
   when the flood destroyed the land,
   he will never forsake you;
   he will swear to you again.

291 Alan J. Price

Tick tock, tick tock.
Life is rather like a clock;
I am like a little wheel,
however big or small I feel;
God can use me in his plan,
I can serve him as I am.
Isn't it good? Isn't it good?

292 From the Missal

Ubi caritas et amor.
Ubi caritas Deus ibi est.

Translation: Where true love and charity are found, God is there.

293 Unknown

1. Vaster far than any ocean,
   deeper than the deepest sea
   is the love of Christ my Saviour,
   reaching through eternity.

2. But my sins are truly many,
   is God's grace so vast, so deep?
   Yes, there's grace o'er sin abounding,
   grace to pardon, grace to keep.

3. Can he quench my thirst for ever?
   Will his Spirit strength impart?
   Yes, he gives me living water,
   springing up within my heart.

294 Scripture

Wait for the Lord, whose day is near.
Wait for the Lord: keep watch, take heart!

295 Marie Lydia Pereira

Wake up, O people, the Lord is very near!
Wake up and stand for the Lord.
Wake up, O people, the Lord is very near!
Wake up and stand for the Lord.

1. Your saving Lord is near. Wake up!
   His glory will appear. Wake up!
   Your hour of grace is nearer than it ever was.

2. The night of sin has passed. Wake up!
   The light is near at last. Wake up!
   The day star, Christ, the Son of God will soon appear.

3. To live in love and peace. Wake up!
   To let all quarrels cease. Wake up!
   To live that all you do may stand the light of day.

4. That Christ may be your shield. Wake up!
   That death to life may yield. Wake up!
   That heaven's gate be opened wide again for you.

296 Estelle White

Walk with me, O my Lord,
through the darkest night
and brightest day.
Be at my side, O Lord,
hold my hand
and guide me on my way.

1. Sometimes the road seems long,
   my energy is spent.
   Then, Lord, I think of you
   and I am given strength.

2. Stones often bar my path
   and there are times I fall,
   but you are always there
   to help me when I call.

3. Just as you calmed the wind
   and walked upon the sea,
   conquer, my living Lord,
   the storms that threaten me.

4. Help me to pierce the mists
   that cloud my heart and mind,
   so that I shall not fear
   the steepest mountainside.

5. As once you healed the lame
   and gave sight to the blind,
   help me when I'm downcast,
   to hold my head up high.

297 Susan Sayers

We are his people, the sheep of his flock,
his people, the sheep of his flock.

1. Shout with gladness to God
   all the earth joyfully obey him.
   Come and gather before him now,
   singing songs of gladness.

2. Understand that the Lord is our God;
   he it is who made us.
   We his people belong to him,
   he our loving shepherd.

3. O how faithful and good is the Lord,
   loving us for ever;
   rich in mercy and faithfulness,
   true through all the ages.

298 Traditional South African, trans. Anders Nyberg

We are marching in the light of God. (4)
We are marching,
Oo, we are marching in the light of God.
We are marching,
Oo, we are marching in the light of God.

To create further verses, 'marching' may be replaced with
'dancing', 'singing', 'praying', and so on.

299 W. L. Wallace

1. We are one family together,
   we are one family in God.
   We are one family together,
   the whole earth is our home.

2. We care for creatures and for plant life,
   we care for everything that lives.
   We care for soil, for air and water,
   the whole earth is our home.

3. We care for children and for adults,
   we care for those who are oppressed.
   We care for justice and for sharing,
   the whole earth is our home.

4. We are one family together,
   we are one family in God.
   We are one family together,
   the whole earth is our home.

300 Tom Leigh

We are the Easter people:
'Alleluia' is our song.
Let us rejoice!
Let us sing out:
'Jesus is risen!
Alleluia, alleluia, alleluia.'

1. He died for us:
   now he is risen.
   We share his life:
   Jesus is Lord!

2. His light shines out,
   dispelling the darkness.
   Tell the whole world:
   Jesus is Lord!

3. Proclaim his glory:
   Christ is the Saviour.
   He dies no more:
   Jesus is Lord!

4. God's people sing!
   You share his victory.
   Have no more fear:
   Jesus is Lord!

301 Carey Landry

1. We believe in God the Father,
   we believe, we believe.
   We believe he is the Holy One,
   we believe, we believe.

2. We believe in Jesus Christ, the Lord,
   we believe, we believe.
   We believe he is God's only Son,
   we believe, we believe.

Continued overleaf

3. He was conceived by the Holy Spirit;
   born of the Virgin Mary.
   For us he died and was buried.
   On the third day he rose again.

4. We believe in the Holy Spirit,
   we believe, we believe.
   We believe in the Holy Church of God,
   we believe, we believe.

5. We believe in God's forgiveness;
   the resurrection from the dead.
   We believe in life everlasting.
   We believe, we believe.
   Amen. We believe.
   Amen. We believe.

302 Michael Forster

1. We can plough and dig the land,
   we can plant and sow,
   we can water, we can weed,
   but we can't make things grow.

   That is something only God can do, (3)
   only God can make things grow.

2. We can edge and we can prune,
   we can rake and hoe,
   we can lift and we can feed,
   but we can't make things grow.

3. We can watch the little shoots
   sprouting row by row,
   we can hope and we can pray,
   but we can't make things grow.

303 Susan Mee

1. We eat the plants that grow from the seed,
   but it's God who gives the harvest.
   Cures can be made from herbs and from weeds,
   but it's God who gives the harvest.
   Everything beneath the sun,
   all the things we claim we've done,
   all are part of God's creation:
   we can meet people's needs
   with things we grow from seed,
   but it's God who gives the harvest.

2. We find the iron and turn it to steel,
   but it's God who gives the harvest.
   We pull the levers, we turn the wheels,
   but it's God who gives the harvest.
   Everything we say we've made,
   plastic bags to metal spades,
   all are part of God's creation:
   we can make lots of things
   from microchips to springs,
   but it's God who gives the harvest.

304 Michael Forster

1. We have a dream: this nation will arise,
   and truly live according to its creed,
   that all are equal in their maker's eyes,
   and none shall suffer through another's greed.

2. We have a dream that one day we shall see
   a world of justice, truth and equity,
   where children of the slaves and of the free
   will share the banquet of community.

3. We have a dream of deserts brought to flower,
   once made infertile by oppression's heat,
   when love and truth shall end oppressive power,
   and streams of righteousness and justice meet.

4. We have a dream: our children shall be free
   from judgements based on colour or on race;
   free to become whatever they may be,
   of their own choosing in the light of grace.

5. We have a dream that truth will overcome
   the fear and anger of our present day;
   that black and white will share a common home,
   and hand in hand will walk the pilgrim way.

6. We have a dream: each valley will be raised,
   and every mountain, every hill brought down;
   then shall creation echo perfect praise,
   and share God's glory under freedom's crown!

305 Fred Kaan

1. We have a King who rides a donkey, (3)
   and his name is Jesus.

   Jesus the King is risen, (3)
   early in the morning.

2. Trees are waving a royal welcome, (3)
   for the King called Jesus.

3. We have a King who cares for people, (3)
   and his name is Jesus.

4. A loaf and a cup upon the table, (3)
   bread-and-wine is Jesus.

5. We have a King with a bowl and towel, (3)
   Servant-King is Jesus.

6. What shall we do with our life this morning? (3)
   Give it up in service!

306 Matthias Claudius, trans. Jane Montgomery Campbell

1. We plough the fields and scatter
   the good seed on the land,
   but it is fed and watered
   by God's almighty hand:
   he sends the snow in winter,
   the warmth to swell the grain,
   the breezes and the sunshine,
   and soft, refreshing rain.

Continued overleaf

All good gifts around us
are sent from heav'n above;
then thank the Lord, O thank the Lord,
for all his love.

2. He only is the maker
   of all things near and far;
   he paints the wayside flower,
   he lights the evening star.
   He fills the earth with beauty,
   by him the birds are fed;
   much more to us, his children,
   he gives our daily bread.

3. We thank thee then, O Father,
   for all things bright and good:
   the seed-time and the harvest,
   our life, our health, our food.
   Accept the gifts we offer
   for all thy love imparts,
   and, what thou most desirest,
   our humble, thankful hearts.

307 John L. Bell and Graham Maule

Lines in ordinary type are sung by the leader; those in bold type by everybody.

1. We're going to shine like the sun
   in the kingdom of heaven,
   shine like the sun
   in the kingdom of heaven;
   we're going to shine like the sun
   in the kingdom of heaven,
   and no one will ever be the same.

And it's all in Jesus' name;
and it's all in Jesus' name;
yes, it's all in Jesus' name
that no one will ever be the same.

2. We're going to learn from the poor
   in the kingdom of heaven,
   learn from the poor . . .

3. We're going to walk with the weak
   in the kingdom of heaven,
   walk with the weak . . .

4. We're going to drink the new wine
   in the kingdom of heaven,
   drink the new wine . . .

5. And it all starts now
   in the kingdom of heaven,
   all starts now . . .

308 Christina Wilde

1. We thank God for the harvest
   we gather ev'ry day,
   the things God grows from seeds we sow
   in all our work and play.

   Gotta get out and scatter some seed,
   grow some crops and smother the weeds,
   so much love there's no room for greed,
   gotta go and scatter some seeds.

Continued overleaf

2. God gives love to be scattered,
   and seeds of faith to sow,
   then sprinkles grace in ev'ry place
   to make the harvest grow.

   Gotta get out and scatter some seed,
   grow some crops and smother the weeds,
   so much love there's no room for greed,
   gotta go and scatter some seeds.

3. We can work all together,
   with people everywhere:
   in every place, each creed and race,
   God gives us love to share.

309   Ian Smale

We will praise, we will praise,
we will praise the Lord,
we will praise the Lord because he is good.
We will praise, we will praise,
we will praise the Lord
because his love is everlasting.

Bring on the trumpets and harps,
let's hear the cymbals ring,
then in harmony
lift our voices and sing, sing.
We will praise, we will praise,
we will praise the Lord,
we will praise the Lord because he is good.
We will praise, we will praise,
we will praise the Lord
because his love is everlasting.

310 Michael Forster

1. What kind of man was this, and how did he offend,
   who taught us love, and lived it to the end;
   who sought the way of truth, all other things above?
   What kind of man was this, what kind of love?

2. What kind of man was this, so full of truth divine,
   who turned the foulest water into wine;
   who called us to his side, and gave us all a place?
   What kind of man was this, what kind of grace?

3. What kind of man was this, who opened up his heart
   to those who sought to tear his flesh apart;
   whose all-forgiving words his perfect nature prove?
   What kind of man was this, what kind of love?

4. What kind of man was this, who helped us all to see
   the fullness of our human dignity?
   So hopeful in despair, so noble in disgrace,
   what kind of man was this, what kind of grace?

311 Willard F. Jabusch

Whatsoever you do
to the least of my brothers,
that you do unto me.

1. When I was hungry you gave me to eat.
   When I was thirsty you gave me to drink.
   Now enter into the home of my Father.

Continued overleaf

2. When I was homeless you opened your door.
   When I was naked you gave me your coat.
   Now enter into the home of my Father.

   Whatsoever you do
   to the least of my brothers,
   that you do unto me.

3. When I was weary you helped me find rest.
   When I was anxious you calmed all my fears.
   Now enter into the home of my Father.

4. When in a prison you came to my cell.
   When on a sick-bed you cared for my needs.
   Now enter into the home of my Father.

5. When I was aged you bothered to smile.
   When I was restless you listened and cared.
   Now enter into the home of my Father.

6. When I was laughed at you stood by my side.
   When I was happy you shared in my joy.
   Now enter into the home of my Father.

312 Paul Booth

1. When God made the garden of creation,
   he filled it full of his love;
   when God made the garden of creation,
   he saw that it was good.
   There's room for you, and room for me,
   and room for everyone:

for God is a Father who loves his children,
and gives them a place in the sun.
When God made the garden of creation,
he filled it full of his love.

2. When God made the hamper of creation,
   he filled it full of his love;
   when God made the hamper of creation,
   he saw that it was good.
   There's food for you, and food for me,
   and food for everyone:
   but often we're greedy, and waste God's bounty,
   so some don't get any at all.
   When God made the hamper of creation,
   he filled it full of his love.

3. When God made the fam'ly of creation,
   he made it out of his love;
   when God made the fam'ly of creation,
   he saw that it was good.
   There's love for you, and love for me,
   and love for everyone:
   but sometimes we're selfish, ignore our neighbours,
   and seek our own place in the sun.
   When God made the fam'ly of creation,
   he made it out of his love.

© Mr Paul Booth

313 Sydney Carter

1. When I needed a neighbour
   were you there, were you there?
   When I needed a neighbour,
   were you there?

Continued overleaf

And the creed and the colour
and the name won't matter,
were you there?

2. I was hungry and thirsty . . .

3. I was cold, I was naked . . .

4. When I needed a shelter . . .

5. When I needed a healer . . .

6. Wherever you travel
   I'll be there, I'll be there,
   wherever you travel
   I'll be there.

   Last refrain:

   And the creed and the colour
   and the name won't matter,
   I'll be there.

© 1965, 1997 Stainer & Bell Ltd.

314 David Palmer

1. When is he coming,
   when, O when is he coming, the Redeemer?
   When will we see him,
   when, O when will we see him, the Redeemer?

   Come, O come, from your kingdom up there,
   from your kingdom up there above!
   Come, O come to your people on earth,
   to your people on earth bring love!
   Emmanuel! Emmanuel! Emmanuel!

2. Long years a-waiting,
   many years here a-waiting the Redeemer!
   Ready to greet him,
   always ready to meet him, the Redeemer!

3. Spare us from evil,
   from the clutches of evil, O Redeemer!
   Though we are sinners
   we have known your forgiveness, O Redeemer!

315 Susan Sayers

1. When Jesus was my age he played with his friends,
   played with his friends, played with his friends;
   when Jesus was my age he played with his friends,
   and he's friends with each one of us now.

2. When Jesus was my age he laughed and he sang,
   laughed and he sang, laughed and he sang;
   when Jesus was my age he laughed and he sang,
   and he loves hearing us singing now.

3. When Jesus was my age he sometimes felt sad,
   sometimes felt sad, sometimes felt sad;
   when Jesus was my age he sometimes felt sad,
   and he shares in our sadnesses now.

4. When Jesus was my age he went to his school,
   went to his school, went to his school;
   when Jesus was my age he went to his school,
   and he goes everywhere with us now.

316 Michael Cockett

1. When the day grows cold,
   when the dark takes hold,
   then I hear you say:
   'Hope will light your way.'

   Loving you gently, Lord,
   knowing you're there,
   finding my hope in you,
   safe in your care. (Repeat)

2. When the petals fall,
   when the winter calls,
   then I think of you,
   faith will rise anew.

   Loving you gently, Lord,
   knowing you're there,
   finding my faith in you,
   safe in your care. (Repeat)

3. When the gale has blown,
   when the storm has torn,
   then the calm recalls
   peace that conquers all.

   Loving you gently, Lord,
   knowing you're there,
   finding my peace in you,
   safe in your care. (Repeat)

317 Unknown

1. When the Spirit of the Lord is within my heart
   I will sing as David sang.
   When the Spirit of the Lord is within my heart
   I will sing as David sang.
   I will sing, I will sing,
   I will sing as David sang.
   I will sing, I will sing,
   I will sing as David sang.

2. When the Spirit of the Lord is within my heart
   I will clap as David clapped . . .

3. When the Spirit of the Lord is within my heart
   I will dance as David danced . . .

4. When the Spirit of the Lord is within my heart
   I will praise as David praised . . .

318 Anne Conlon

1. When your Father made the world,
   before that world was old,
   in his eye what he had made was lovely to behold.
   Help your people to care for your world.

   The world is a garden you made,
   and you are the one who planted the seed,
   the world is a garden you made,
   a life for our food, life for our joy,
   life we could kill with our selfish greed.

Continued overleaf

2. All the world that he had made,
the seas, the rocks, the air,
all the creatures and the plants he gave into our care.
Help your people to care for your world.

The world is a garden you made,
and you are the one who planted the seed,
the world is a garden you made,
a life for our food, life for our joy,
life we could kill with our selfish greed.

3. When you walked in Galilee,
you said your Father knows
when each tiny sparrow dies, each fragile lily grows.
Help your people to care for your world.

4. And the children of the earth,
like sheep within your fold,
should have food enough to eat, and shelter from
the cold.
Help your people to care for your world.

319 John Glynn

Where are you bound, Mary, Mary?
Where are you bound, Mother of God?

1. Beauty is a dove
sitting on a sunlit bough,
beauty is a pray'r
without the need of words.
Words are more than sounds
falling off an empty tongue:
let it be according to his word.

2. Mary heard the word
   spoken in her inmost heart.
   Mary bore the Word
   and held him in her arms.
   Sorrow she has known,
   seeing him upon the cross;
   greater joy to see him rise again.

3. Where are we all bound,
   carrying the word of God?
   Time and place are ours
   to make his glory known.
   Mary bore him first,
   we will tell the whole wide world:
   let it be according to his word.

320 Graham Kendrick

1. Whether you're one or whether you're two
   or three or four or five,
   six or sev'n or eight or nine,
   it's good to be alive.
   It really doesn't matter how old you are,
   Jesus loves you whoever you are.

   la la la la la la la la la,
   Jesus loves us all.
   La la la la la la la la la,
   Jesus loves us all.

Continued overleaf

2. Whether you're big or whether you're small,
   or somewhere in between,
   first in the class or middle or last,
   we're all the same to him.
   It really doesn't matter how clever you are,
   Jesus loves you whoever you are.

   la la la la la la la la la,
   Jesus loves us all.
   La la la la la la la la la,
   Jesus loves us all.

321 Susan Sayers

Lines in ordinary type are sung by the leader; those in bold type by everybody.

1. Who made the corn grow?
   Who made the corn grow?
   God made the corn grow.
   God made the corn grow.
   Why did he do so?
   To feed all his children on earth.

2. Who made the beans grow?
   Who made the beans grow?
   God made the beans grow.
   God made the beans grow.
   Why did he do so?
   To feed all his children on earth.

3. Who made the fruit grow?
   Who made the fruit grow?

God made the fruit grow.
God made the fruit grow.
Why did he do so?
To feed all his children on earth.

4. Who made the carrots grow?
   Who made the carrots grow?
   God made the carrots grow.
   God made the carrots grow.
   Why did he do so?
   To feed all his children on earth.

5. Who made the yams grow?
   Who made the yams grow?
   God made the yams grow.
   God made the yams grow.
   Why did he do so?
   To feed all his children on earth.

322 Paul Booth

1. Who put the colours in the rainbow?
   Who put the salt into the sea?
   Who put the cold into the snowflake?
   Who made you and me?
   Who put the hump upon the camel?
   Who put the neck on the giraffe?
   Who put the tail upon the monkey?
   Who made hyenas laugh?
   Who made whales and snails and quails?
   Who made hogs and dogs and frogs?
   Who made bats and rats and cats?
   Who made everything?

Continued overleaf

2. Who put the gold into the sunshine?
   Who put the sparkle in the stars?
   Who put the silver in the moonlight?
   Who made Earth and Mars?
   Who put the scent into the roses?
   Who taught the honey bee to dance?
   Who put the tree inside the acorn?
   It surely can't be chance!
   Who made seas and leaves and trees?
   Who made snow and winds that blow?
   Who made streams and rivers flow?
   God made all of these!

© Mr Paul Booth

323 Unknown

Who's the king of the jungle?
Who's the king of the sea?
Who's the king of the universe,
and who's the king of me?
I'll tell you:
J-E-S-U-S is.
He's the king of me:
he's the king of the universe,
the jungle and the sea.

324 Unknown

With Jesus in the boat we can smile at the storm,
smile at the storm,
smile at the storm.
With Jesus in the boat we can smile at the storm,
as we go sailing home.

Sailing, sailing home,
sailing, sailing home.
With Jesus in the boat we can smile at the storm,
as we go sailing home.

325 Dan Schutte

Yahweh, I know you are near,
standing always at my side.
You guard me from the foe
and you lead me in ways everlasting.

1. Lord, you have searched my heart,
   and you know when I sit and when I stand,
   for your hand is upon me, protecting me from death,
   keeping me from harm.

2. Where can I run from your love?
   If I climb to the heavens, you are there.
   If I fly to the sunrise or sail beyond the sea,
   still I'd find you there.

3. You know my heart and its ways,
   you who formed every hollow of my being,
   in the secret of darkness, before I saw the sun
   in my mother's womb.

4. Great and renowned are your works;
   how profound and exalted are your thoughts,
   even if I could count them, they number as the stars,
   you would still be there.

326 Unknown

Yesterday, today, for ever, Jesus is the same;
all may change, but Jesus never,
glory to his name!
Glory to his name! Glory to his name!
All may change, but Jesus never,
Glory to his name!

327 Mavis Ford

You are the King of glory,
you are the Prince of peace,
you are the Lord of heav'n and earth,
you're the Son of righteousness!
Angels bow down before you,
worship and adore,
for you have the words of eternal life,
you are Jesus Christ the Lord!
Hosanna to the Son of David!
Hosanna to the King of kings!
Glory in the highest heaven,
for Jesus the Messiah reigns.

© Word's Spirit of Praise Music/CopyCare

328 Susan Sayers

1. You can drink it, swim in it,
   cook and wash up in it,
   fish can breathe in it,
   what can it be?

It's water!
God has provided us water!
Water of life.

2. It's as hard as rock,
   yet it flows down a mountain,
   and clouds drop drips of it –
   what can it be?

3. It's as light as snowflakes
   and heavy as hailstones,
   as small as dewdrops
   and big as the sea.

329 Steffi Geiser Rubin and Stuart Dauermann

You shall go out with joy
and be led forth with peace,
and the mountains and the hills
shall break forth before you.
There'll be shouts of joy
and the trees of the field
shall clap, shall clap their hands.
And the trees of the field
shall clap their hands,
and the trees of the field
shall clap their hands,
and the trees of the field
shall clap their hands,
and you'll go out with joy.

330 Traditional

1. You've got to move when the Spirit says move,
   You've got to move when the Spirit says move,
   'cause when the Spirit says move,
   you've got to move when the Spirit,
   move when the Spirit says move.

2. You've got to sing when the Spirit says sing . . .

3. You've got to clap when the Spirit says clap . . .

4. You've got to shout when the Spirit says shout . . .

331 Unknown

Zacchaeus was a very little man,
and a very little man was he.
He climbed up into a sycamore tree,
for the Saviour he wanted to see.
And when the Saviour passed that way,
he looked into the tree and said,
'Now Zacchaeus, you came down,
for I'm coming to your house for tea.'

332 Sue McClellan, John Paculabo and Keith Ryecroft

Zip bam boo, zama lama la boo,
there's freedom in Jesus Christ.
Zip bam boo, zama lama la boo,
there's freedom in Jesus Christ.
Though we hung him on a cross till he died in pain,
Three days later he's alive again.
Zip bam boo, zama lama la boo,
there's freedom in Jesus Christ.

1. This Jesus was a working man
   who shouted 'Yes' to life,
   but didn't choose to settle down,
   or take himself a wife.
   To live for God he made his task,
   'Who is this man?' the people ask.
   Zip bam boo, zama lama la boo,
   there's freedom in Jesus Christ.

2. He'd come to share good news from God
   and show that he is Lord.
   He made folk whole who trusted him
   and took him at his word.
   He fought oppression, loved the poor,
   gave the people hope once more.
   Zip bam boo, zama lama la boo,
   there's freedom in Jesus Christ.

3. 'He's mad! He claims to be God's Son
   and give new life to men!
   Let's kill this Christ, once and for all,
   no trouble from him then!'
   'It's death then, Jesus, the cross for you!'
   Said, 'Man, that's what I came to do!'
   Zip bam boo, zama lama la boo,
   there's freedom in Jesus Christ.

CAROLS

Carols

333   Graham Kendrick

At this time of giving,
gladly now we bring
gifts of goodness and mercy
from a heav'nly King.

1. Earth could not contain the treasures
   heaven holds for you,
   perfect joy and lasting pleasures,
   love so strong and true.

2. May his tender love surround you
   at this Christmastime;
   may you see his smiling face
   that in the darkness shines.

3. But the many gifts he gives
   are all poured out from one;
   come, receive the greatest gift,
   the gift of God's own Son.

   Last two refrains and verses

   Lai, lai, lai, etc.

334 William James Kirkpatrick

1. Away in a manger,
   no crib for a bed,
   the little Lord Jesus
   laid down his sweet head.
   The stars in the bright sky
   looked down where he lay,
   the little Lord Jesus,
   asleep on the hay.

2. The cattle are lowing,
   the baby awakes,
   but little Lord Jesus
   no crying he makes.
   I love thee, Lord Jesus!
   Look down from the sky,
   and stay by my side
   until morning is nigh.

3. Be near me, Lord Jesus;
   I ask thee to stay
   close by me for ever,
   and love me, I pray.
   Bless all the dear children
   in thy tender care,
   and fit us for heaven,
   to live with thee there.

   Alternative version of verses 2 and 3
   Michael Forster

2. The cattle are lowing,
   they also adore
   the little Lord Jesus
   who lies in the straw.

I love you, Lord Jesus,
I know you are near
to love and protect me
till morning is here.

3. Be near me, Lord Jesus,
I ask you to stay
close by me for ever,
and love me, I pray.
Bless all the dear children
in your tender care,
prepare us for heaven,
to live with you there.

335 Geoffrey Ainger

1. Born in the night, Mary's child,
a long way from your home;
coming in need, Mary's child,
born in a borrowed room.

2. Clear shining light, Mary's child,
your face lights up our way;
light of the world, Mary's child,
dawn on our darkened day.

3. Truth of our life, Mary's child,
you tell us God is good;
prove it is true, Mary's child,
go to your cross of wood.

4. Hope of the world, Mary's child,
you're coming soon to reign;
King of the earth, Mary's child,
walk in our streets again.

336 Valerie Collison

Come and join the celebration.
It's a very special day.
Come and share our jubilation;
there's a new King born today.

1. See, the shepherds
   hurry down to Bethlehem,
   gaze in wonder,
   at the Son of God who lay before them.

2. Wise men journey,
   led to worship by a star,
   kneel in homage,
   bringing precious gifts from lands afar. So:

3. 'God is with us,'
   round the world the message bring.
   He is with us,
   'Welcome,' all the bells on earth are pealing.

337 John Glynn

1. Come, Christian people,
   take heed what I say:
   Here, in this stable,
   your King was born today.

   Star of wisdom, child of gladness,
   tell him all your troubles.
   Mary's boy has banished sadness,
   why be sorrowful now?

2. Not much to look at
   – simply straw and hay –
   yet on that carpet
   your King was laid today.

3. World, are you listening?
   Take heed what I say:
   Here on this planet
   your King still lives today.

338 Unknown, alt.

Come, come, come to the manger,
children, come to the children's King;
sing, sing, chorus of angels,
star of morning o'er Bethlehem sing.

1. He lies 'mid the beasts of the stall,
   who is Maker and Lord of us all;
   the wintry wind blows cold and dreary,
   see, he weeps, the world is weary;
   Lord, have pity and mercy on me!

2. He leaves all his glory behind,
   to be born and to die for mankind,
   with grateful beasts his cradle chooses,
   thankless world his love refuses;
   Lord, have pity and mercy on me!

3. To the manger of Bethlehem come,
   to the Saviour Emmanuel's home;
   the heav'nly hosts above are singing,
   set the Christmas bells a-ringing;
   Lord, have pity and mercy on me!

339

1. Come, they told me, pah-rum-pum-pum-pum!
   our new born King to see, pah-rum-pum-pum-pum!
   Our finest gifts we bring, pah-rum-pum-pum-pum!
   to lay before our King, pah-rum-pum-pum-pum!
   Rum-pum-pum-pum! Rum-pum-pum-pum!
   So, to honour him, pah-rum-pum-pum-pum!
   when we come.

2. Baby Jesus, pah-rum-pum-pum-pum!
   I am a poor child too, pah-rum-pum-pum-pum!
   I have no gift to bring, pah-rum-pum-pum-pum!
   that's fit to give a King, pah-rum-pum-pum-pum!
   Rum-pum-pum-pum! Rum-pum-pum-pum!
   Shall I play for you, pah-rum-pum-pum-pum!
   on my drum?

3. Mary nodded, pah-rum-pum-pum-pum!
   The ox and lamb kept time, pah-rum-pum-pum-pum!
   I played my drum for him, pah-rum-pum-pum-pum!
   I played my best for him, pah-rum-pum-pum-pum!
   Rum-pum-pum-pum! Rum-pum-pum-pum!
   Then he smiled at me, pah-rum-pum-pum-pum!
   me and my drum.

340 George Ratcliffe Woodward

1. Ding dong, merrily on high!
   in heav'n the bells are ringing;
   ding dong, verily the sky
   is riv'n with angels singing.

   Gloria, hosanna in excelsis!

2. E'en so here below, below,
   let steeple bells be swungen,
   and io, io, io,
   by priest and people sungen.

3. Pray you, dutifully prime
   your matin chime, ye ringers;
   may you beautifully rhyme
   your evetime song, ye singers.

341 Sarah Forth

Everyone's a Christmas baby,
everyone's a Christmas child.
We've got Jesus as a brother,
we've got Mary as a mother,
yes, everyone's a Christmas child.

1. Every new-born human child
   is a sign of hope and joy,
   and God is smiling up at us
   from every girl and boy. Yes!

2. Christmas comes on every day,
   and in every kind of place,
   for each new child that's born on earth
   reveals God's love and grace. Yes!

3. Life and hope begin anew
   when another child is born,
   and every morning that we wake
   is like a new world's dawn. Yes!

1. God was born on earth, a homeless stranger,
   facing every kind of mortal danger,
   scrounged himself a bed in a donkey's manger
   in the town of Bethlehem.

   Never mind the sheep, look for the baby,
   that's what the angel said!
   Never mind the sheep, look for the baby,
   with a manger for his bed.

2. Shepherds in the fields with sheep to care for,
   angels said, 'What are you sitting there for?
   Never mind the questions, the whys and wherefores,
   get along to Bethlehem!'

3. 'Never mind the sheep, look for the baby,
   he's the one to watch, I don't mean maybe.
   If you want to share in this special day, be
   sure to go to Bethlehem.'

4. So they left the sheep and went out looking,
   eager to find out what God had cooking,
   found a classic problem of overbooking
   in the town of Bethlehem.

5. Jesus doesn't put on airs and graces,
   likes to be in unexpected places,
   comes to us in smiles and in warm embraces,
   as he did at Bethlehem.

343 Spiritual

Go, tell it on the mountain,
over the hills and everywhere.
Go tell it on the mountain
that Jesus Christ is born.

1. While shepherds kept their watching
   o'er wand'ring flocks by night,
   behold, from out of heaven,
   there shone a holy light.

2. And lo, when they had seen it,
   they all bowed down and prayed;
   they travelled on together
   to where the babe was laid.

3. When first I was a seeker,
   I sought both night and day;
   I asked the Lord to help me
   and he showed me the way.

4. He set me as a watchman
   upon the city wall,
   and if I am a Christian,
   I am the least of all.

344 Charles Wesley, George Whitfield, Martin Madan and others, alt.

1. Hark, the herald-angels sing
   glory to the new-born King;
   peace on earth and mercy mild,
   God and sinners reconciled:
   joyful, all ye nations rise,
   join the triumph of the skies,
   with th'angelic host proclaim,
   'Christ is born in Bethlehem.'

Continued overleaf

Hark, the herald-angels sing
glory to the new-born King.

2. Christ, by highest heav'n adored,
   Christ, the everlasting Lord,
   late in time behold him come,
   offspring of a virgin's womb!
   Veiled in flesh the Godhead see,
   hail, th'incarnate Deity!
   Pleased as man with us to dwell,
   Jesus, our Emmanuel.

3. Hail, the heav'n-born Prince of Peace!
   Hail, the Sun of Righteousness!
   Light and life to all he brings,
   ris'n with healing in his wings;
   mild he lays his glory by,
   born that we no more may die,
   born to raise us from the earth,
   born to give us second birth.

345 Graham Kendrick

Heaven invites you to a party,
to celebrate the birth of a Son;
angels rejoicing in the starlight,
singing, 'Christ your Saviour has come.'
(Repeat)

And it's for you (and it's for you)
and it's for me (and it's for me),
for all your friends (for all your friends)
and family (and family).

Now heaven's door (now heaven's door)
is open wide (is open wide),
so come on in (so come on in),
come, step inside (come, step inside).

Angels from the realms of glory,
wing your flight o'er all the earth;
you who sang creation's story,
now proclaim Messiah's birth.

And it's for you (and it's for you)
and it's for me (and it's for me),
for all your friends (for all your friends)
and family (and family).

Let trumpets blast (let trumpets blast),
let music play (let music play),
let people shout (let people shout),
let banners wave (let banners wave).

Come, all you people (come, all you people),
Join hands together (join hands together),
Bring all your neighbours
(bring all your neighbours),
everybody! (everybody!)

Send invitations (send invitations)
to every nation (to every nation),
come and adore him (come and adore him),
everybody! (everybody!)
everybody! (everybody!)

Heaven invites you to a party,
to celebrate the birth of a Son;
angels rejoicing in the starlight,
singing, 'Christ your Saviour has come.'

Continued overleaf

And it's for you (and it's for you)
and it's for me (and it's for me),
for all your friends (for all your friends)
and family (and family).

Let trumpets blast (let trumpets blast),
let music play (let music play),
let people shout (let people shout),
let banners wave (let banners wave).

346 Michael Forster

Hee, haw! Hee, haw!
Doesn't anybody care?
There's a baby in my dinner
and it's just not fair!

1. Jesus in the manger,
   lying in the hay,
   far too young to realise he's getting in the way!
   I don't blame the baby,
   not his fault at all,
   but his parents should respect a donkey's
       feeding stall!

2. After all that journey,
   with my heavy load,
   did I ever once complain about the dreadful road?
   I can cope with backache,
   and these swollen feet.
   All I ask is some respect, and one square meal to eat.

3. 'Be prepared,' I told them,
   'better book ahead.'
   Joseph said, 'Don't be an ass,' and took a chance
        instead.
   Now they've pinched my bedroom,
   People are so rude!
   I can cope with that, but not a baby in my food!

347 Christina Rossetti

1. In the bleak midwinter
   frosty wind made moan,
   earth stood hard as iron,
   water like a stone;
   snow had fallen, snow on snow,
   snow on snow,
   in the bleak midwinter, long ago.

2. Our God, heav'n cannot hold him
   nor earth sustain;
   heav'n and earth shall flee away
   when he comes to reign.
   In the bleak midwinter
   a stable place sufficed
   the Lord God almighty, Jesus Christ.

3. Enough for him, whom cherubim
   worship night and day,
   a breastful of milk,
   and a mangerful of hay:
   enough for him, whom angels
   fall down before,
   the ox and ass and camel which adore.

Continued overleaf

4. Angels and archangels
   may have gathered there,
   cherubim and seraphim
   thronged the air;
   but only his mother
   in her maiden bliss
   worshipped the beloved with a kiss.

5. What can I give him,
   poor as I am?
   If I were a shepherd
   I would bring a lamb;
   if I were a wise man
   I would do my part,
   yet what I can I give him: give my heart.

348 John Jacob Niles

1. I wonder as I wander out under the sky,
   how Jesus the Saviour did come for to die
   for poor ord'n'ry people like you and like I.
   I wonder as I wander out under the sky.

2. When Mary birthed Jesus, 'twas in a cow's stall
   with wise men and farmers and shepherds and all.
   But high from God's heaven a star's light did fall,
   and the promise of ages it did then recall.

3. If Jesus had wanted for any wee thing,
   a star in the sky or a bird on the wing,
   or all of God's angels in heav'n for to sing,
   he surely could have it, 'cause he was the King.

349 Isaac Watts, alt.

1. Joy to the world! The Lord is come;
   let earth receive her King;
   let every heart prepare him room,
   and heav'n and nature sing,
   and heav'n and nature sing,
   and heav'n, and heav'n and nature sing.

2. Joy to the earth! The Saviour reigns;
   let us our songs employ;
   while fields and floods, rocks, hills and plains
   repeat the sounding joy,
   repeat the sounding joy,
   repeat, repeat the sounding joy.

3. He rules the world with truth and grace,
   and makes the nations prove
   the glories of his righteousness,
   and wonders of his love,
   and wonders of his love,
   and wonders, wonders of his love.

350 Mick Gisbey

Light a flame within my heart that's burning bright:
fan the fire of joy in me to set the world alight.
Let my flame begin to spread, my life to glow:
God of light, may I reflect your love to all I know.

1. From heaven's splendour
   he comes to earth,
   while all the angels
   celebrate the good news of his birth.

Continued overleaf

2. We too exalt you,
   our glorious King:
   Jesus our Saviour
   Paid the price to take away our sin.

   Light a flame within my heart that's burning bright:
   fan the fire of joy in me to set the world alight.
   Let my flame begin to spread, my life to glow:
   God of light, may I reflect your love to all I know.

© *1987 Kingsway's Thankyou Music*

351 Eric Boswell

1. Little donkey, little donkey,
   on the dusty road,
   got to keep on plodding onwards,
   with your precious load.
   Been a long time, little donkey,
   through the winter's night;
   don't give up now, little donkey,
   Bethlehem's in sight.

   Ring out those bells tonight,
   Bethlehem, Bethlehem,
   follow that star tonight,
   Bethlehem, Bethlehem.
   Little donkey, little donkey,
   had a heavy day,
   little donkey, carry Mary safely on her way.

2. Little donkey, little donkey,
   on the dusty road,
   there are wise men, waiting for a
   sign to bring them here.
   Do not falter, little donkey,
   there's a star ahead;
   it will guide you, little donkey,
   to a cattle shed.

352 Spiritual, alt

1. Mary had a baby, yes, Lord.
   Mary had a baby, yes, my Lord.
   Mary had a baby, yes, Lord.
   And God became a human being just like me.

2. What did she name him?

3. Mary named him Jesus.

4. Where was he born?

5. Born in a stable!

6. Where did she lay him?

7. Laid him in a manger.

353 Michael Forster

1. Mary said to Joseph,
   'Let's find a place to stay,
   for it's much too cold to sleep outside
   with a baby on the way!'

   There wasn't any room at the inn.
   There wasn't any room at the inn.
   They couldn't find a bed
   for a weary mother's head
   in the whole of Bethlehem!

2. Joseph said to Mary,
   'I hope we'll find a place,
   but the town is full of visitors
   and there's not a lot of space.'

3. Then they found a stable,
   a simple little shed,
   and the Saviour of the world was born
   with a manger for his bed!

354 John Francis Wade, trans. Frederick Oakeley and others

1. O come, all ye faithful,
   joyful and triumphant,
   O come ye, O come ye to Bethlehem.
   Come and behold him,
   born the king of angels:

   O come, let us adore him,
   O come, let us adore him,
   O come, let us adore him,
   Christ the Lord.

2. God of God,
   Light of Light,
   lo, he abhors not the virgin's womb;
   very God,
   begotten, not created:

3. Sing, choir of angels,
   sing in exultation,
   sing, all ye citizens of heav'n above;
   glory to God
   in the highest:

4. Yea, Lord, we greet thee,
   born this happy morning,
   Jesu, to thee be glory giv'n;
   Word of the Father,
   now in flesh appearing:

355 Phillips Brooks, alt

1. O little town of Bethlehem,
   how still we see thee lie!
   Above thy deep and dreamless sleep
   the silent stars go by.
   Yet in thy dark streets shineth
   the everlasting light;
   the hopes and fears of all the years
   are met in thee tonight.

2. For Christ is born of Mary;
   and, gathered all above,
   while mortals sleep, the angels keep
   their watch of wondering love;
   O morning stars, together
   proclaim the holy birth,
   and praises sing to God the King,
   and peace upon the earth.

Continued overleaf

3. How silently, how silently,
   the wondrous gift is giv'n!
   So God imparts to human hearts
   the blessings of his heav'n.
   No ear may hear his coming;
   but in this world of sin,
   where meek souls will receive him, still
   the dear Christ enters in.

4. O holy child of Bethlehem,
   descend to us, we pray;
   cast out our sin and enter in,
   be born in us today.
   We hear the Christmas angels
   the great glad tidings tell:
   O come to us, abide with us,
   our Lord Emmanuel.

356 Cecil Francis Alexander/Michael Forster (v. 4)

1. Once in royal David's city
   stood a lowly cattle shed,
   where a mother laid her baby
   in a manger for his bed:
   Mary was that mother mild,
   Jesus Christ her little child.

2. He came down to earth from heaven,
   who is God and Lord of all,
   and his shelter was a stable,
   and his cradle was a stall;
   with the humble, poor and lowly,
   lived on earth our Saviour holy.

3. And through all his wondrous childhood,
   day by day like us he grew;
   he was little, weak and helpless,
   tears and smiles like us he knew;
   and he feeleth for our sadness,
   and he shareth in our gladness.

4. Still, among the poor and lowly,
   hope in Christ is brought to birth,
   with the promise of salvation
   for the nations of the earth;
   still in him our life is found,
   and our hope of heav'n is crowned.

5. And our eyes at last shall see him,
   through his own redeeming love,
   for that child, so dear and gentle,
   is our Lord in heav'n above;
   and he leads his children on
   to the place where he is gone.

Verse 4 © 1996 Kevin Mayhew Ltd.

357 Traditional

1. On Christmas night all Christians sing,
   to hear the news the angels bring,
   on Christmas night all Christians sing,
   to hear the news the angels bring,
   news of great joy, news of great mirth,
   news of our merciful King's birth.

Continued overleaf

2. Then why should we on earth be so sad,
   since our Redeemer made us glad,
   then why should we on earth be so sad,
   since our Redeemer made us glad,
   when from our sin he set us free,
   all for to gain our liberty?

3. When sin departs before his grace,
   then life and health come in its place,
   when sin departs before his grace,
   then life and health come in its place,
   angels and earth with joy may sing,
   all for to see the new-born King.

4. All out of darkness we have light,
   Which made the angels sing this night:
   all out of darkness we have light,
   Which made the angels sing this night:
   'Glory to God and peace to men,
   now and for evermore. Amen.'

358 Edward Caswall

1. See, amid the winter's snow,
   born for us on earth below,
   see, the tender Lamb appears,
   promised from eternal years.

   Hail, thou ever blessed morn,
   hail, redemption's happy dawn!
   Sing through all Jerusalem,
   Christ is born in Bethlehem.

2. Lo, within a manger lies
   he who built the starry skies;
   he who, throned in heights sublime,
   sits amid the cherubim.

3. Say, ye holy shepherds, say,
   what your joyful news today?
   Wherefore have ye left your sheep
   on the lonely mountain steep?

4. 'As we watched at dead of night,
   lo, we saw a wondrous light;
   angels, singing peace on earth,
   told us of the Saviour's birth.'

5. Sacred infant, all divine,
   what a tender love was thine,
   thus to come from highest bliss,
   down to such a world as this!

6. Virgin mother, Mary blest,
   by the joys that fill thy breast,
   pray for us, that we may prove
   worthy of the Saviour's love.

359 Michael Perry

1. See him lying on a bed of straw,
   a draughty stable with an open door,
   Mary cradling the babe she bore:
   the Prince of Glory is his name.

   O now carry me to Bethlehem,
   to see the Lord of love again:
   just as poor as was the stable then,
   the Prince of Glory when he came!

2. Star of silver, sweep across the skies,
   show where Jesus in a manger lies;
   shepherds, swiftly from your stupor rise
   to see the Saviour of the world!

Continued overleaf

3. Angels, sing again the song you sang,
   sing the story of God's gracious plan,
   sing that Bethl'em's little baby can
   be the Saviour of us all.

   O now carry me to Bethlehem,
   to see the Lord of love again:
   just as poor as was the stable then,
   the Prince of Glory when he came!

4. Mine are riches from your poverty;
   from your innocence, eternity;
   mine, forgiveness by your death for me,
   child of sorrow for my joy.

360 Joseph Mohr, trans. John Freeman Young

1. Silent night, holy night.
   All is calm, all is bright,
   round yon virgin mother and child,
   holy infant, so tender and mild:
   sleep in heavenly peace,
   sleep in heavenly peace.

2. Silent night, holy night.
   Shepherds quake at the sight,
   glories stream from heaven afar,
   heav'nly hosts sing alleluia:
   Christ the Saviour is born,
   Christ the Saviour is born.

3. Silent night, holy night.
   Son of God, love's pure light,
   radiant beams from thy holy face,
   with the dawn of redeeming grace:
   Jesus, Lord, at thy birth,
   Jesus, Lord, at thy birth.

361 Sabine Baring-Gould

1. Sing lullaby!
   Lullaby baby, now reclining,
   sing lullaby!
   Hush, do not wake the infant King.
   Angels are watching, stars are shining
   over the place where he is lying:
   sing lullaby!

2. Sing lullaby!
   Lullaby baby, now a-sleeping,
   sing lullaby!
   Hush, do not wake the infant King.
   Soon will come sorrow with the morning,
   soon will come bitter grief and weeping:
   sing lullaby!

3. Sing lullaby!
   Lullaby baby, now a-dozing,
   sing lullaby!
   Hush, do not wake the infant King.
   Soon comes the cross, the nails, the piercing,
   then in the grave at last reposing:
   sing lullaby!

Continued overleaf

4. Sing lullaby!
   Lullaby! is the babe awaking?
   Sing lullaby!
   Hush, do not stir the infant King,
   dreaming of Easter, gladsome morning,
   conquering death, its bondage breaking:
   sing lullaby!

362 Sabine Baring-Gould

1. The angel Gabriel from heaven came,
   his wings as drifted snow, his eyes as flame.
   'All hail,' said he, 'thou lowly maiden, Mary,
   most highly favoured lady.' Gloria!

2. 'For known a blessèd mother thou shalt be.
   All generations laud and honour thee.
   Thy Son shall be Emmanuel, by seers foretold,
   most highly favoured lady.' Gloria!

3. Then gentle Mary meekly bowed her head.
   'To me be as it pleaseth God,' she said.
   'My soul shall laud and magnify his holy name.'
   Most highly favoured lady! Gloria!

4. Of her, Emmanuel the Christ was born
   in Bethlehem, all on a Christmas morn;
   and Christian folk throughout the world will ever say:
   'Most highly favoured lady.' Gloria!

363 From William Sandys' *Christmas Carols Ancient and Modern*

1. The first nowell the angel did say
   was to certain poor shepherds in fields as they lay;
   in fields where they lay, keeping their sheep,
   on a cold winter's night that was so deep.

   *Nowell, nowell, nowell, nowell,
   born is the King of Israel!*

2. They lookèd up and saw a star,
   shining in the east, beyond them far,
   and to the earth it gave great light,
   and so it continued both day and night.

3. And by the light of that same star,
   three wise men came from country far;
   to seek for a king was their intent,
   and to follow the star wherever it went.

4. This star drew nigh to the north-west,
   o'er Bethlehem it took its rest,
   and there it did both stop and stay
   right over the place where Jesus lay.

5. Then entered in those wise men three,
   full rev'rently upon their knee,
   and offered there, in his presence,
   their gold and myrrh and frankincense.

6. Then let us all with one accord
   sing praises to our heav'nly Lord,
   that hath made heav'n and earth of naught,
   and with his blood mankind hath bought.

364 Traditional

1. The holly and the ivy,
   when they are both full grown,
   of all the trees that are in the wood
   the holly bears the crown.

   The rising of the sun,
   and the running of the deer,
   the playing of the merry organ,
   sweet singing in the choir.

2. The holly bears a blossom
   as white as the lily flow'r,
   and Mary bore sweet Jesus Christ
   to be our sweet Saviour.

3. The holly bears a berry
   as red as any blood,
   and Mary bore sweet Jesus Christ
   to do poor sinners good.

4. The holly bears a prickle
   as sharp as any thorn,
   and Mary bore sweet Jesus Christ
   on Christmas Day in the morn.

5. The holly bears a bark
   as bitter as any gall,
   and Mary bore sweet Jesus Christ
   for to redeem us all.

6. The holly and the ivy,
   when they are both full grown,
   of all the trees that are in the wood
   the holly bears the crown.

365 Spiritual

1. There's a star in the east on Christmas morn,
   rise up, shepherd, and follow.
   It will lead to the place where the Saviour's born,
   rise up, shepherd, and follow.

   Leave your sheep and leave your lambs,
   O rise up, shepherd, and follow.
   Leave your ewes and leave your rams,
   O rise up, shepherd, and follow.
   Follow, follow, rise up, shepherd, and follow.
   Follow the star of Bethlehem,
   rise up, shepherd, and follow.

2. If you take good heed of the angel's words,
   rise up, shepherd, and follow,
   you'll leave your flocks, you'll forget your herds,
   rise up, shepherd, and follow.

366 Traditional West Indian

1. The Virgin Mary had a baby boy,
   the Virgin Mary had a baby boy,
   the Virgin Mary had a baby boy,
   and they said that his name was Jesus.

   He came from the glory,
   he came from the glorious kingdom.
   He came from the glory,
   he came from the glorious kingdom.
   O yes, believer. O yes, believer.
   He came from the glory,
   he came from the glorious kingdom.

Continued overleaf

2. The angels sang when the baby was born, (3)
   and proclaimed him the Saviour Jesus.

   He came from the glory,
   he came from the glorious kingdom.
   He came from the glory,
   he came from the glorious kingdom.
   O yes, believer. O yes, believer.
   He came from the glory,
   he came from the glorious kingdom.

3. The wise men saw where the baby was born, (3)
   and they saw that his name was Jesus.

367 Graham Kendrick

1. This child secretly comes in the night,
   oh this child, hiding a heavenly light,
   oh this child coming to us like a stranger,
   this heavenly child.

   This child, heaven come down now to be with us here,
   heavenly love and mercy appear,
   softly in awe and wonder come near
   to this heavenly child.

2. This child, rising on us like the sun,
   oh this child, given to light everyone,
   oh this child, guiding our feet on the pathway
   to peace on earth.

3. This child, raising the humble and poor,
   oh this child, making the proud ones to fall;
   this child, filling the hungry with good things,
   this heavenly child.

368 John Henry Hopkins

1. We three kings of Orient are;
   bearing gifts we traverse afar;
   field and fountain, moor and mountain,
   following yonder star.

   O star of wonder, star of night,
   star with royal beauty bright;
   westward leading, still proceeding,
   guide us to thy perfect light.

2. Born a King on Bethlehem plain,
   gold I bring to crown him again,
   King for ever, ceasing never
   over us all to reign.

3. Frankincense to offer have I,
   incense owns a Deity nigh,
   prayer and praising gladly raising,
   worship him, God most high.

4. Myrrh is mine, its bitter perfume
   breathes a life of gathering gloom;
   sorrowing, sighing, bleeding, dying,
   sealed in the stone-cold tomb.

5. Glorious now behold him arise,
   King and God and sacrifice;
   alleluia, alleluia,
   earth to heav'n replies.

369 Traditional

1. We wish you a merry Christmas,
   we wish you a merry Christmas,
   we wish you a merry Christmas,
   and a happy new year!

   Good tidings we bring
   to you and your kin;
   we wish you a merry Christmas
   and a happy new year!

2. Now bring us some figgy pudding,
   now bring us some figgy pudding,
   now bring us some figgy pudding,
   and bring some out here.

3. We all like figgy pudding,
   we all like figgy pudding,
   we all like figgy pudding,
   so bring some out here.

4. We won't go until we've got some,
   we won't go until we've got some,
   we won't go until we've got some,
   so bring some out here.

370 Graham Kendrick

1. What kind of greatness can this be,
   that chose to be made small,
   exchanging untold majesty,
   for a world so pitiful?
   That God should come as one of us,
   I'll never understand.
   The more I hear the story told,
   the more amazed I am.

Oh, what else can I do,
but kneel and worship you,
and come just as I am,
my whole life an offering.

2. The one in whom we live and move
   in swaddling cloths lies bound.
   The voice that cried, 'Let there be light',
   asleep without a sound.
   The one who strode among the stars,
   and called each one by name,
   lies helpless in a mother's arms
   and must learn to walk again.

3. What greater love could he have shown
   to shamed humanity?
   Yet human pride hates to believe
   in such deep humility.
   But nations now may see his grace
   and know that he is near,
   when his meek heart, his words, his works
   are incarnate in us here.

371 Nahum Tate

1. While shepherds watched their flocks by night,
   all seated on the ground,
   the angel of the Lord came down,
   and glory shone around.

2. 'Fear not,' said he (for mighty dread
   had seized their troubled mind);
   'glad tidings of great joy I bring
   to you and all mankind.

Continued overleaf

3. 'To you, in David's town this day,
    is born, of David's line,
    a Saviour who is Christ the Lord;
    and this shall be the sign:

4. 'The heav'nly babe you there shall find
    to human view displayed,
    all meanly wrapped in swathing bands
    and in a manger laid.'

5. Thus spake the seraph, and forthwith
    appeared a shining throng
    of angels praising God, who thus
    addressed their joyful song.

6. 'All glory be to God on high
    and to the earth be peace;
    good will from heav'n to all the world
    begin and never cease.'

MUSIC FOR THE MASS

Music for the Mass

372 from the Mass

Lord, have mercy.
Christ, have mercy.
Lord, have mercy,
have mercy on us.

373 from the Mass

Lord, have mercy.
Lord, have mercy.
Lord, have mercy.

Christ, have mercy.
Christ, have mercy.
Christ, have mercy.

Lord, have mercy.
Lord, have mercy.
Lord, have mercy.

374 from the Mass

Lord, have mercy.
Lord, have mercy.
Lord, have mercy.
Lord, have mercy.

Continued overleaf

Christ, have mercy.
Christ, have mercy.
Christ, have mercy.
Christ, have mercy.

Lord, have mercy.
Lord, have mercy.
Lord, have mercy.
Lord, have mercy.

375   Gordon Rock

Lord, have mercy on my soul;
Lord, have mercy on my soul;
Lord, have mercy,
Lord, have mercy,
Lord, have mercy on my soul.

Christ, have mercy on my soul;
Christ, have mercy on my soul;
Christ, have mercy,
Christ, have mercy,
Christ, have mercy on my soul.

Pray for me, pray for me,
brothers and sisters, pray for me.

I confess that I have sinned,
sinned in thought and word and deed,
done the things I should not do,
left undone what I should do.

Blessed Mary, pray for me;
Saints and angels, pray for me;
brothers and sisters,
brothers and sisters,
pray for me to the Lord our God.
Lord, have mercy on my soul;
Lord, have mercy on my soul.

© *Gordon Rock*

376 Michael Forster

1. Lord, have mercy on us,
   hear us as we pray;
   Lord, have mercy on us,
   take our sin away.

2. Christ, have mercy on us,
   hear us as we pray;
   Christ, have mercy on us,
   take our sin away.

3. Lord, have mercy on us,
   hear us as we pray;
   Lord, have mercy on us,
   take our sin away.

© *1997 Kevin Mayhew Ltd.*

377 from the Mass

Kyrie, Kyrie, eleison.

378 Mike Anderson

*Gloria (clap, clap), gloria (clap, clap),
in excelsis Deo.
Gloria (clap, clap), gloria (clap, clap),
in excelsis Deo.*

1. Lord God, heavenly King,
   peace you bring to us;
   we worship you, we give you thanks,
   we sing our song of praise.

2. Jesus, Saviour of all,
   Lord God, Lamb of God,
   you take away our sins, O Lord,
   have mercy on us all.

3. At the Father's right hand,
   Lord, receive our prayer,
   for you alone are the Holy One,
   and you alone are Lord.

4. Glory, Father and Son,
   glory, Holy Spirit,
   to you we raise our hands up high,
   we glorify your name.

379 Michael Forster

1. Glory and honour to God in the highest,
   and peace to all his people, his people on earth.
   God of creation,
   Father of nations,
   glory, thanksgiving and praise are your worth.

2. Lord Jesus Christ, only Son of the Father,
   O Lamb of God who takes our transgression away,
   grant us your healing,
   mercy revealing,
   seated in glory, O hear us we pray.

3. You, only you, are the Lord high and holy,
   with God the Holy Spirit exalted above.
   O perfect union,
   blessed Communion!
   Reign with the Father in glory and love.

380 Danny Daniels

Glory, glory in the highest;
glory to the Almighty;
glory to the Lamb of God,
and glory to the living Word;
glory to the Lamb!
(Repeat)

I give glory (glory),
glory (glory),
glory, glory to the Lamb!
I give glory (glory),
glory (glory),
glory, glory to the Lamb!
I give glory to the Lamb!

Glory, glory to God,
glory to God in the highest;
peace to his people on earth,
peace to his people on earth.
Lord God, heavenly King,
almighty God and Father,
we worship you, we give you thanks,
we praise you for your glory.
Glory, glory to God,
glory to God in the highest;
peace to his people on earth,
peace to his people on earth.

Lord Jesus Christ,
only Son of the Father,
Lord God, Lamb of God,
you take away the sin of the world,
have mercy upon us;
you are seated at the right hand of the Father,
receive our prayer,
receive our prayer,
receive our prayer.

You alone are the Holy One,
you alone are the Lord,
you alone are the Lord,
you alone are the Most High,
Jesus Christ,
with the Holy Spirit,
in the glory, the glory,
the glory of God the Father.
Amen, amen, amen,
amen, amen, amen.

Lines in ordinary type are sung by the leader; those in bold type by everybody.

1. Glory to God, glory to God,
    Glory to the Father.
    Glory to God, glory to God,
    Glory to the Father.

    To him be glory for ever.
    To him be glory for ever.
    Alleluia, amen.
    Alleluia, amen, alleluia, amen,
    alleluia, amen.

2. Glory to God, glory to God,
    Son of the Father.
    Glory to God, glory to God,
    Son of the Father.

3. Glory to God, glory to God,
    Glory to the Spirit.
    Glory to God, glory to God,
    Glory to the Spirit.

383 Michael Forster

1. Glory to God, to God in the height,
   bringing peace to ev'ry nation.
   Lord God almighty, Father and King,
   and the author of salvation.
   'Glory!' let the people sing,
   let the whole creation ring,
   telling out redemption's story,
   as we worship your name
   with thankful songs of praise
   for the love that is your glory.

2. Jesus, the Father's one holy Son,
   all creation bows before you.
   You are the God, the God we acclaim,
   and we worship and adore you.
   Lamb of God, to you we pray,
   you who take our sin away,
   mercy, grace and truth revealing.
   At the right hand of God,
   receive our humble prayer
   for forgiveness, hope and healing.

3. You, Jesus Christ, alone are the Lord,
   by your own eternal merit;
   sharing by right the glory of God
   in the presence of the Spirit.
   You alone are Lord Most High,
   you alone we glorify,
   reigning over all creation.
   To the Father, the Son
   and Spirit, three in one,
   be eternal acclamation.

384 Michael Forster

1. Sing glory to God in the height of the heavens,
   salvation and peace to his people on earth;
   our King and our Saviour, our God and our Father,
   we worship and praise you and sing of your worth.

   Creation unites in the pow'r of the Spirit,
   in praise of the Father, through Jesus, the Son.
   So complex, so simple, so clear, so mysterious,
   our God ever three yet eternally one.

2. Lord Jesus, the Christ, only Son of the Father,
   the Lamb who has carried our burden of shame,
   now seated on high in the glory of heaven,
   have mercy upon us who call on your name.

3. For you, only you, we acknowledge as holy,
   we name you alone as our Saviour and Lord;
   you only, O Christ, with the Spirit exalted,
   at one with the Father, for ever adored.

385 Francesca Leftley

1. Sing to God a song of glory,
   peace he brings to all on earth.
   Worship we the King of heaven;
   praise and bless his holy name.

   Glory, glory, sing his glory.
   Glory to our God on high.

2. Sing to Christ, the Father's loved one,
   Jesus, Lord and Lamb of God:
   hear our prayer, O Lord, have mercy,
   You who bear the sins of all.

Continued overleaf

3. Sing to Christ, the Lord and Saviour,
   seated there at God's right hand:
   hear our prayer, O Lord, have mercy,
   you alone the Holy One.

   Glory, glory, sing his glory.
   Glory to our God on high.

4. Glory sing to God the Father,
   glory to his only Son,
   glory to the Holy Spirit,
   glory to the three in one.

© 1978 Kevin Mayhew Ltd.

386 from the Roman Missal

Gloria, gloria
in excelsis Deo!
Gloria, gloria,
alleluia, alleluia!

387 Michael Forster

1. Holy, most holy, all holy the Lord,
   in power and wisdom for ever adored!
   The earth and the heavens are full of your love;
   our joyful hosannas re-echo above!

2. Blessèd, most blessèd, all blessèd is he
   whose life makes us whole and whose death sets
       us free;
   who comes in the name of the Father of light,
   let endless hosannas resound in the height!

© 1995 Kevin Mayhew Ltd.

388 Michael Forster

Holy, most holy, all holy the Lord,
God of all pow'r and might;
heaven and earth with your glory abound,
wrapped in eternal light.
Blessed is he, he who has come,
come in the Father's name,
Servant and Lord, Saviour and Judge,
making his royal claim.
Holy, most holy, all holy the Lord,
God of all pow'r and might;
now with hosannas and jubilant praise,
earth and the heav'ns unite.

389 from the Roman Missal

Holy, holy Lord,
holy, holy Lord,
Lord God of power,
Lord God of might,
holy, holy Lord.
Heaven and earth,
heaven and earth
are full, are full of your glory.
Hosanna, hosanna,
hosanna in the highest.

Blessed is he,
blessed is he who comes
in the name of the Lord.
Hosanna, hosanna,
hosanna in the highest.

390 from the Roman Missal

Holy, holy, holy Lord,
God of power and God of might.
Heaven and earth are full of your glory.
Hosanna in the highest,
hosanna, hosanna,
hosanna in the highest,
hosanna, hosanna,
hosanna in the highest.

Blessed is he, blessed is he,
blessed is he who comes in the name,
he who comes in the name of the Lord.
Hosanna in the highest,
hosanna, hosanna,
hosanna in the highest,
hosanna, hosanna,
hosanna in the highest.

391 John Ballantine

1. Holy, holy, holy is the Lord,
   holy is the Lord God almighty!
   Holy, holy, holy is the Lord,
   holy is the Lord God almighty!
   Who was and is, and is to come;
   Holy, holy, holy is the Lord.

2. Blessèd, blessèd, blest is he who comes,
   blest is he who comes in the Lord's name.
   Blessèd, blessèd, blest is he who comes,
   blest is he who comes in the Lord's name.
   Hosanna in the heights of heav'n.
   Blessèd, blessèd, blessèd is the Lord.

392 from the Roman Missal

Christ has died.
Christ is risen.
Christ will come again.

393 from the Roman Missal

Christ has died, alleluia.
Christ is risen, alleluia.
Christ will come again,
alleluia, alleluia.

394 from the Roman Missal

When we eat this bread and drink this cup,
we proclaim your death, Lord Jesus,
until you come in glory,
until you come in glory.

395 from the Roman Missal

1. Lamb of God,
   you take away the sins of the world:
   have mercy on us,
   have mercy on us.

2. Lamb of God,
   you take away the sins of the world:
   have mercy on us,
   have mercy on us.

Continued overleaf

3. Lamb of God,
   you take away the sins of the world:
   grant us peace,
   grant us peace.

396 from the Roman Missal

Lamb of God,
you take away the sins of the world;
have mercy on us.

Lamb of God,
you take away the sins of the world;
have mercy on us.

Lamb of God,
you take away the sins of the world;
grant us peace.

397 Michael Forster

1. O Lamb of God, come cleanse our hearts
   and take our sin away.
   O Lamb of God, your grace impart,
   and let our guilty fear depart,
   have mercy, Lord, we pray,
   have mercy, Lord, we pray.

2. O Lamb of God, our lives restore,
   our guilty souls release.
   Into our lives your Spirit pour
   and let us live for evermore
   in perfect heav'nly peace,
   in perfect heav'nly peace.

398 from the Roman Missal

Jesus, Lamb of God,
you take away the sins of the world;
have mercy, mercy on us,
have mercy on us, Lord Jesus.

Jesus, Lamb of God,
you take away the sins of the world;
have mercy, mercy on us,
have mercy on us, Lord Jesus.

Jesus, Lamb of God,
you take away the sins of the world;
grant us, grant us peace,
grant us peace, Lord Jesus.

399 from the Roman Missal

Jesus, Lamb of God,
Jesus, Lamb of God,
you take away the sins of the world;
have mercy on us.

Jesus, Lamb of God,
Jesus, Lamb of God,
you take away the sins of the world;
have mercy on us.

Jesus, Lamb of God,
Jesus, Lamb of God,
you take away the sins of the world;
grant us your peace;
grant us your peace.

400 The American Eucharist, adapted from the Liturgy
by Sandra Joan Billington

Kyrie

1. Lord, have mercy; Lord, have mercy;
   on your servants, Lord, have mercy.
   God Almighty, just and faithful,
   Lord, have mercy; Lord, have mercy.

2. Christ, have mercy; Christ, have mercy;
   gift from heaven, Christ, have mercy.
   Light of truth and light of justice,
   Christ, have mercy; Christ, have mercy.

3. Lord, have mercy; Lord, have mercy;
   on your servants, Lord, have mercy.
   God Almighty, just and faithful,
   Lord, have mercy; Lord, have mercy.

Sanctus

1. Holy, holy, holy, holy,
   Lord of hosts. You fill with glory
   all the earth and all the heavens.
   Sing hosanna, sing hosanna.

2. Blest and holy, blest and holy,
   he who comes now in the Lord's name.
   In the highest sing hosanna,
   in the highest sing hosanna.

Agnus Dei

1. Jesus, Lamb of God, have mercy,
   bearer of our sins, have mercy.
   Jesus, Lamb of God, have mercy,
   bearer of our sins, have mercy.

2. Saviour of the world, Lord Jesus,
   may your peace be with us always.
   Saviour of the world, Lord Jesus,
   may your peace be with us always.

401 The Hopwood Mass, adapted from the Liturgy by Terence Collins

Kyrie

1. Father of all, O Lord, have mercy.
   Father of all, O Lord, have mercy.
   Father of all, have mercy on us.
   Father of all, be ever near us.

2. Saviour of all, O Christ, have mercy.
   Saviour of all, O Christ, have mercy.
   Saviour of all, have mercy on us.
   Saviour of all, be ever near us.

3. Spirit of all, O Lord, have mercy.
   Spirit of all, O Lord, have mercy.
   Spirit of all, have mercy on us.
   Spirit of all, be ever near us.

Sanctus

1. Holy are you, Lord of creation!
   Holy are you, Lord God of angels!
   Holy are you, God of all people!
   Heaven and earth proclaim your glory.

2. Glory to you! Your name is holy.
   Blessèd is he who comes in your name!
   Glory to him! We sing his praises.
   Heaven and earth proclaim your glory.

Agnus Dei

O Lamb of God, you bore our sinning.
O Lamb of God, you bore our dying.
O Lamb of God, have mercy on us.
O Lamb of God, your peace be with us.

402 The Israeli Mass, adapted from the Liturgy
by Anthony Hamson

Kyrie

1. Lord, have mercy. Lord, have mercy.
   Lord, have mercy on us all.
   Lord, have mercy. Lord, have mercy.
   Lord, have mercy on us all.

2. Christ, have mercy. Christ, have mercy.
   Christ, have mercy on us all.
   Christ, have mercy. Christ, have mercy.
   Christ, have mercy on us all.

3. Lord, have mercy. Lord, have mercy.
   Lord, have mercy on us all.
   Lord, have mercy. Lord, have mercy.
   Lord, have mercy on us all.

Sanctus

1. Holy, holy, holy, holy,
   Lord of pow'r, Lord of might.
   Heav'n and earth are filled with glory.
   Sing hosanna evermore.

2. Blest and holy, blest and holy,
   he who comes from God on high.
   Raise your voices, sing his glory,
   praise his name for evermore.

Agnus Dei

1. Lamb of God, you take away the sin,
   the sin of all the world:
   give us mercy, give us mercy,
   give us mercy, Lamb of God.

2. Lamb of God, you take away the sin,
   the sin of all the world:
   give us mercy, give us mercy,
   give us mercy, Lamb of God.

3. Lamb of God, you take away the sin,
   the sin of all the world:
   grant us peace, Lord; grant us peace, Lord;
   grant us peace, O Lamb of God.

INDEXES

Index of First Lines

An extensive Index of Uses and a Scriptural Index
may be found in the full music edition.

Stories and Characters from the Bible

Acknowledgements

The publishers wish to express their gratitude to the following for permission to include copyright material in this publication. Details of copyright owners are given underneath each individual hymn.

Ateliers et Presses de Taizé, F-7 1250 Taizé-Communauté, France.

Mike Anderson, 83 Denholme, Upholland, Lancs, WN8 0AX.

Belmont Abbey, Hereford, HR2 9RZ.

Central Board of Finance of the Church of England, Church House, Great Smith Street, London, SW1P 3NZ.

Geoffrey Chapman (Cassell plc), 125 Strand, London, WC2R 0BB.

Church of the Messiah, 231 East Grand Boulevard, Detroit, Michigan 48207, USA.

J. Curwen & Sons Ltd (Chester Music Ltd), 8/9 Frith Street, London, W1V 5TZ.

CopyCare Ltd, PO Box 77, Hailsham, East Sussex, BN27 3EF, UK, on behalf of Word of God Music; Mercy/Vineyard Publishing/Music Services; Bud John Songs/EMI Christian Music Publishing; Maranatha! Music; Singspiration Music/Universal Songs; Zondervan Corporation/Universal Songs; Sacred Songs/Word music; Salvationist Publishing & Supplies; Birdwing Music/BMG Songs Inc (Ears To Hear Music/EMI Christian Music Publishing); Word's Spirit of Praise Music; Lillenas Publishing Co and Mission Hills Music. Used by permission.

Daybreak Music (ICC Studios), Silverdale Road, Eastbourne, East Sussex, BN20 7AB.

GIA Publications Inc, 7404 S. Mason Avenue, Chicago, Illinois 60638, USA. All rights reserved. Used by permission.

David Higham Associates, 5/8 Lower John Street, Golden Square, London, W1R 4HA.

High-Fye Music Ltd (Campbell, Connelly & Co Ltd), 8/9 Frith Street, London, W1V 5TZ.

International Music Publications Ltd, Southend Road, Woodford Green, Essex, 1G8 8HN, England.

Iona Community, Pearce Institute, 840 Govan Road, Glasgow, G51 3UU, Scotland.

Rev Willard F. Jabusch, Calvert House, 5735 South University, Chicago, Illinois 60637, USA.

Jubilate Hymns, 4 Thorne Park Road, Chelston, Torquay, TQ2 6RX.

Kingsway's Thankyou Music, PO Box 75, Eastbourne, East Sussex, BN23 6NW, UK, on behalf of Kingsway's Thankyou Music; Scripture in Song /Integrity Music; Integrity's Hosanna!; Fred Bock Music Company, Europe (excl Germany) and British Commonwealth (excl Canada); Glorie Music, Worldwide; Celebration, Europe and British Commonwealth (excl Canada, Australasia and Africa); Mission Hills Music; Stuart K. Hine, Worldwide (excl USA and Canada) and David C. Cook Co. Used by permission.

Make Way Music, PO Box 263, Croydon, CR9 5AP. All rights reserved. Used by permission.

McCrimmon Publishing Co Ltd, 10/12 High Street, Great Wakering, Southend-on-Sea, Essex, SS3 0EQ.

Medical Mission Sisters, 92 Sherman Street, Hartford, CT 06105, USA.

OCP Publications, 5536 NE Hassalo, Portland, OR 97213 USA. All rights reserved.

Oxford University Press, Great Clarendon Street, Oxford, OX2 6DP.

Society of the Sacred Heart, 4389 West Pine Boulevard, St Louis, Missouri 63108, USA.

Restoration Music Ltd, PO Box 356, Leighton Buzzard, Beds, LU7 8WP.

Scripture Press Publications Inc, 1825 College Avenue, Wheaton, Illinois 60187-4498, USA.

Scripture Union, 207/209 Queensway, Bletchley, Milton Keynes, MK2 2EB.

Sea Dream Music, 236 Sebert Road, Forest Gate, London, E7 0NP.

Sisters of Mary of Namur, 3000 Lansing, Wichita Falls, Texas 76309, USA. All rights reserved. Used by permission.

SPCK, Holy Trinity Church, Marylebone Road, London, NW1 4DU.

Stainer & Bell Ltd, PO Box 110, Victoria House, 23 Gruneisen Road, Finchley, London, N3 1DZ.

A. P. Watt, 20 John Street, London, WC1N 2DR.

Joseph Weinberger Ltd, 12/14 Mortimer Street, London, W1N 7RD.

Word of Life International, PO Box 2322, Burleigh MDC, Queensland 4220, Australia.